God in His mercy and His love is warning us.
He is calling out to all of us in the body of Christ
to be a holy people
and to come to Him with all of our hearts.

207 End-Time Prophecies and Dreams

200 Prophecies and 7 Dreams:
What God is saying to Christians and
the Church.

THE LAST CALL

The Preparation of the Bride for The Rapture of the Church

Compiled and Edited by R.C. Schaffter

A Clarion Call Publication

The Last Call ©1994 is a companion volume to
Prophecies of the End-Times ©1992

The Last Call
Published and Distributed by:
The Clarion Call
P.O. Box 335
Lannon, Wisconsin 53046

Copyright ©1994 by:
R. C. Schaffter
All Rights Reserved

Printed in U.S.A.
ISBN: 0-9633026-1-2

Unless otherwise indicated, all Scripture verses that are referenced are from the King James Version of the Bible. The word "see" before a reference means that the quotation is very close to, but not identical to, the indicated Scripture verse. Brackets around words "[. . .]" indicate that those words have been inserted by the editor.

Acknowledgments

Thanks to the following yielded vessels of the Lord who permitted the word that God gave them to be included in this book:

Barbara Bloedow	Gwen R. Shaw
Frances J. Roberts	Lance Lambert
Dumitru Duduman	Daniel Lundstrom
Father Michael Scanlan	Kathleen Bojanowski
Sister Francis Clare	Charles Bernardi
James P. Corbett	Jane Cage

Anna Schrader

Thanks also to Ron Auch for allowing the revelation that God gave him to be used in this book.

My sincere appreciation and special thanks go to Gwen Shaw, founder and president of End-Time Handmaidens, for allowing fourteen of the prophecies that God has given her to be used in this book. They came mainly from two of her books, *Day by Day* and *Daily Preparations for Perfection,* and from the *End-Time Handmaidens Magazine.*

Special thanks also go to the following:

Freda Lindsay, Chairman of the Board of Christ for the Nations, for permission to use excerpts from the Anna Schrader prophecy books (12 volumes).

Dumitru Duduman for one prophecy and six dreams from his ministry newsletter, *Hand of Help;* and for a dream from his book, *Through the Fire Without Burning.*

Frances J. Roberts for two prophecies from her books, *Come Away My Beloved* and *On The High Road of Surrender.*

Father Michael Scanlan, T.O.R., President of The Franciscan University of Steubenville, for the word that God gave him at a National Service Committee Meeting of the Catholic Charismatic Renewal.

Timothy Dudley, president of New Leaf Press, for the long prophecy received by Sister Francis Clare, from her book *We, the Bride.*

James Corbett, founder and director of Heir Force Ministries, for a collection of prophecies which were either read on Milwaukee area radio station WKSH or were published in the ministry newsletter, *The Heir Force Herald.*

Ron Auch, founder of Pray-Tell Ministries, for his commentary about the Church, which was originally published in his newsletter, *Pray-Tell Ministries.*

Charles Bernardi for three prophecies which came from his publication, *Perfect Way Newsletter.*

The helpful suggestions, timely encouragement, and prayers of the people who were involved with this project is greatly appreciated.

Table of Contents

Introduction

The book you are about to read, except for two selections, is totally and directly from God. It is a book of prophecies and dreams: revelations from God given to spiritually sensitive, yielded vessels of the Lord by the Holy Spirit. The prophecies and dreams were given to these yielded vessels when, or just after, they were in an attitude of prayer. The prophecies came to them in the form of words. These words were either written down or were spoken out, as they were being received. Those that were spoken were recorded on tape. For the dreams, a description of each one was also written down or recorded, along with any words impressed by God upon the heart of the individual receiving the dream.

This book is a collection of 207 such prophecies and dreams — 200 prophecies and 7 dreams. The yielded vessels that God used for receiving them are listed in the "Acknowledgments." They received these messages and dreams from God in a number of different settings, including: at home in their own prayer closets, in prayer meetings, in regular Sunday morning church services, and, in some cases, at Christian retreats.

For *The Last Call*, the 200 prophecies and 7 dreams were gathered together, prayerfully arranged and grouped according to the main theme of each, and one- to four-line statements or phrases were written for each group. Thus there is a continuous flow and a steady progression of thought and meaning in *The Last Call*, from the very first prophecy on page 12 to the very last one on page 257.

One important note: It must be understood that much of what is called "prophecy" in the Church today is not true Bible prophecy at all. A great deal of what passes for prophecy comes from the flesh — the carnal mind — and is not from the Holy Spirit. Other prophecies do come from the Holy Spirit, but because of the spiritual condition and limitations of the receiving vessel are incomplete and shallow. Still others come from both the Holy Spirit and the flesh. This results in an impure mixture, an impure message.

Some prophecies come from the Holy Spirit and are spiritually sound and complete but are intended for encouragement and comfort only, and nothing else. This is known as exhortation prophecy. It is very common in the public assemblies of most charismatic and pentecostal churches. However, this type of prophecy is also shallow, and a constant, exclusive diet of this kind alone will never adequately feed a church body. Unfortunately, in the majority of charismatic and pentecostal churches, this is usually the highest level of prophecy that ever comes forth, and even that level is reached just part of the time.

The last category, and the one that occurs the least but is needed by the Church the most, is revelation prophecy. It requires a greater degree of yielding on the part of the person receiving the message. Revelation prophecy reveals more of the true heart and mind and nature of God — the riches of His depths and His ways, with nothing impure added and nothing pure missing. Revelation prophecy teaches, guides, corrects, rebukes, nourishes, builds up, warns, and tells of things to come. If heeded, it will totally transform a church or a people of God. That is the kind of prophecy that was selected for this book. Therefore, what you will see and what you will experience as you read the prophecies in this book, will be all God, fully God, and only God. *The Last Call* is a book in which God Speaks.   — R.C.S.

Forward

This book is meant for every Christian, but because of God's strong message to His people in these End-Times, parts of it may be hard to read. Therefore, some individuals might be more comfortable with the book if they read in the central section first; that is, pages 92-98 and pages 123-133. Here God speaks tenderly with a loving heart to His people, drawing them to Himself, calling out to those who truly desire a closer walk with Him and want to be the bride of Jesus Christ.

It is sincerely hoped that everyone reading this book will understand and receive the total statement that God is making to the Church and to His people in these Last Days.

"He who has an ear, let him hear what the Spirit says to the Churches." (Revelation 3:22)

"Surely the Lord God will do nothing
but He reveals His secret to His servants, the prophets.

The Lion has roared, who will not fear?
The Lord God has spoken, who can but prophesy?"

(Amos 3:7,8)

1. To All Christians:

THE LAST CALL

Are You Ready?

The Rapture Call

The call to come as Jesus returns and comes for His bride will be familiar to the bride. The call to come away is the call that the bride has heard and responded to many times: "Come away, My love, My fair one. Rise up, My love, and come away. Come with Me from Lebanon, My spouse. Come, My beloved, let us go forth into the field. The Spirit and the bride say, come! Let him that is athirst come, and whosoever will, let him come and drink of the water of life freely."

The Rapture call will be a clear, loud, clarion call; and the heart of the bride will respond to it. Come away, My love, My dove, My undefiled one.

The Last Call

Soon, My beloved, the last call, the final call will be given. Only those whose hearts have been prepared will be ready to answer it. Only those who have surrendered all of their hearts to Me will be ready to enter into the Marriage Supper of the Lamb. The last call will be given: "Behold, the Bridegroom cometh; go ye out to meet Him." Only those wise virgins equipped and ready will rise up and enter in. The door will then be shut.

The last call will come in a very dark time — a time when the love of many will be waxing cold. The allurement and sin of the world will have enticed, ensnared, deceived, and drawn away many. Their half-hearted love for Me will be clearly evident when the last call is given. The flame of love that will be burning brightly in the vessels of the wise, will have gone out in the vessels of the foolish. Oh, the horror of that day to realize how foolish they have been. Oh, the heartbreak of lukewarm love. Oh, the despair, to be forever separated and shut out!

The hour is late, My beloved. The darkness deepens. It is an urgent hour — an hour to be awake and alert. It is the time to prepare and cast off the works of darkness and put on the armor of light. It is the time now to zealously repent and answer My call of love to come out and separate yourselves unto Me and Me alone, to lay aside the things of the world. It is the time to cleanse and purify your heart and hands.

O My children, will you not come and let Me shine the light of My Word on your heart? Will you not allow Me to search, know, and try your heart and thoughts? Will you not seek Me with all of your heart? Will you not leave your other loves and come to Me with all of your heart? Oh, the hour is so late. So many of you are foolish. You are spending your oil and treasure on your other loves. You have a harlot's heart!

Return to Me. Leave your lovers, and return to Me. I will gather you in My arms and love you freely. Come to Me. Come to Me with all of your heart. Answer now this call of love. It is a call to return to your "first love," your bridal love — extravagant, lavish, spendthrift, doesn't-count [consider]-the-cost, intimate love. There is a price to pay for this love, and you must pay it now. It is the surrender of your whole heart to Me.

Will you not answer My call now, My beloved, and come to the secret closet of love, and prepare your heart and ready yourself for the last call? The last call is the RAPTURE CALL. Only those whose hearts are burning with the flame of first love will be ready and prepared to answer that call.

Will You Rise in the Rapture?
or
Will You be Left Behind?

Come to Me poor — not hanging on to the things of this life, not clinging to them. Give them all to Me — like the widow that cast in all she had. Come and stand before Me empty handed, as it were, with only yourself to offer and give. Come meekly and humbly. I will not refuse you. I will give you what you need, what you lack.

You will rise in the Rapture as you are free of earthly entanglements, earthly weights, earthly baggage. IF YOU CLING TO ANYTHING HERE, IT WILL TIE YOU DOWN!

You are still holding on very tightly to the things of this life. Loosen your grip; let go! The things you hold so tightly with your hands are in reality what your heart loves and treasures. For where your treasure is, there will your heart be also. It is imperative that you let go of all earthly loves and treasures, for they will tie you down and weigh you down and keep you from rising up to meet Me in the air when the last call is given.

You will not rise to meet Me if your hands are holding onto any other love or treasure. You must let go now; you must become unencumbered now. You must seek and desire Me as your only love and greatest treasure. You must cling to Me alone. Let go and abandon all else now. Rid yourself of all that your heart and hands are tied to, or you will not be ready for My soon return — you will not rise in the Rapture!

14

Are You Ready and Watching?

And what will you do in this midnight hour, Church? Will you be ready and watching? Will your lamps be trimmed and burning brightly when the cry resounds: "Behold, the Bridegroom cometh"? Or will you be unprepared? Will you be surprised and shocked when you find you have no oil? Will you finally realize the urgency of the hour? Will you panic when you find you cannot borrow another's oil? Where will you buy? Who will sell? Will you dance your way down the street, with your robes flowing, with those who are ready, or will you run frantically to find the oil so necessary to light your lamp?

You Are Not Ready to Go[1]

How is it, My beloved bride, that you have not been careful to make yourself ready to meet your Beloved? You have not submitted to the heavenly "beauticians." You have rejected the myrrh of suffering which is needed in your life to crush and break your will so that you can accept My will for your life. And you have refused the anointing perfume that comes through the fragrance of a life spent in intimacy with Me, your Beloved.

I am ready to come for you and take you to Myself so that where I am, there you may be also — but you are not ready to go! Your heart is still cleaving to the things of this world. You are like Lot's wife. You still love your cities that are doomed to fiery judgment and destruction. Lot's wife lived only for herself. She was the influence for evil in the life of her husband. She loved the riches and the social life that Sodom offered her. She encouraged her daughters to marry the sons of the prosperous families of Sodom. That is why she looked back.

Let that which happened to her be a warning to you, My beloved. I sent My angels to bring her out. They even took her by the hand and led her out, but still her heart was attached to a doomed city. My bride is still attached to a doomed world. The judgment has begun to fall! Flood, fire, earthquake, wars, famine, pestilence, and all the evil that has befallen you has still not been able to turn your heart back to Me. You still cleave to this doomed world! You still love the temporal more than the eternal.

My beloved, I grieve because you have lost your first love for Me. I have sent out My messengers to bid you to come to My wedding feast, but you have made many excuses and have hardened your heart to My call of love. I cannot plead forever for you to come into My arms. My Father will not permit it. Soon it will be too late, and you will have missed your last opportunity to answer My call.

What will you do then? What will you do when those who are ready have gone into the Marriage Feast and you have been left behind? Even those whom you despise and refuse to recognize or have fellowship with will come into the Kingdom ahead of some of you who think you are so righteous and take pride in the recognition of the religious societies of this world. You love it when other men praise you and honor you and welcome you into their midst. But what good will it do you if you are shut out of the Kingdom of God and refused entrance into the Banqueting Hall of the Marriage Supper of the Lamb?

These are the Last Days. The last call is going out now. Hasten to hear it and to allow My Holy Spirit to do His work in you so that you will not be left behind to taste the evil that will befall the earth very shortly. For know this, that the good people suffer with the evil when the judgment of God falls upon a nation. Not all the people of San Francisco were wicked when the great earthquake and fire destroyed that city. There were also good people who suffered with the wicked. Not all the people who suffered in Hurricane Andrew were wicked. Many were My children. Nor are all the many thousands of people who are suffering in the great floods of central USA wicked. Many are good and innocent people, but they lived where the wicked lived. And after the Rapture takes place, those who are left, even if they are good people, will suffer with the wicked.

So prepare yourself now to be My bride, for soon the call will go out, "Behold, the Bridegroom cometh; go ye out to meet Him!" and then only the wise virgins, who have prepared for that event, will be taken out. The foolish virgins will be left behind to taste the sorrows and sufferings that shall befall as darkness closes in upon a sin-cursed world.

Are You Prepared?

Do you see the order and sequence of the events concerning My first coming? — appearing in different ways, to the shepherds first of all and then to the wise men. Each came to pay their homage and respect, recognizing Me as the coming and promised Messiah. After the shepherds' visit, Mary and Joseph went to the temple to present Me, according to the law and order of the temple. It was then I sent My faithful servants to see the birth of their constant prayers; I revealed My Son to two when they were watching and waiting and persevering in regard to My coming.

So My word to you, My children, is: Watch for My coming with expectant and believing hearts. For as you are faithful and believing, you shall also see Me revealed. You shall see the outpouring of My Spirit, the reviving of My people; and you, My bride, shall behold Me, your beloved Bridegroom. You shall hear Me call you unto Myself: "Rise up, My love, rise up."

Readiness involves obedience in every area. Whatever

you allow to be taken lightly or run over because of your own human reasoning and understanding will cause you to sleep and be unprepared. You are overlooking and passing over many things as being unimportant and of no significance. Pride is keeping you from doing My will in many areas of your life.

The cry of your heart must be: "Come, come My Beloved, come." If it is not, you will not see Me. You are not ready. You are not prepared. Your heart is adulterous!

2. Many Changes Are Coming

Are You Prepared for Them?

Changes

There is a removing and a sifting and a sorting among you that I have ordered and ordained. Many changes are coming. It is according to My plan and purpose. All things will be as I have ordained. Many necessary things will occur in the near future. Do not be upset or shaken by what you see. Some things will affect you personally. You will feel uprooted and abandoned. Be aware that these changes are coming.

Cling fast and hold tightly to Me. I am your Rock and Firm Foundation. I change not. Persevere in prayer. Seek My face as never before and believe that I will keep you in My will as you focus and concentrate on Me and Me alone. The enemy of your soul is right now waging his greatest battle against your mind. He seeks to distract and bind you. He seeks to lead you astray.

Cling fast; hold tightly. Follow My instructions. I am teaching you how to die to yourself and all fleshly desires and loves. It is the only way of victory. It is the only way you will be My prepared bride. Look not at the things or people around you. Look to Me and only Me. Desire Me and Me alone. Do not be deceived by the things around you. Put your trust, faith, and confidence in Me and Me alone. All else will fail you.

Listen, watch, wait. Prepare your heart. I'm coming soon to catch away My beloved, prepared bride.

God's Final Showdown

The final curtain, the final showdown, is about to occur. Men's hearts will fail them in this final hour. Fear will grip the hearts of men and women, young and old, as the curtain falls. They will have no place to run and hide because they have not made Me their secret hiding place. As My judgment begins to fall and the devastation begins, they will run to hide but will find no covering or place of safety.

They have refused and rejected My call and My wooing. They have spurned Me and gone on in their own stubborn, willful ways. They trust in their familiar things and rest in what has always been. They heed not My voice. They tune Me out and shut Me off and comfort themselves in what has always been.

Suddenly things will change. The very system of things will be shaken and upset. Who will they cling to then when all they have ever known has crumbled and nothing is left of the familiar?

Run to Me now; cling to Me now; forsake all for Me now; lay your life down now; hide in Me now. Heed My voice now — as I cry in mercy for you to come. Do not resist any longer. Come, come while there is still time!

Things Are Accelerating

Things are not going to be the way they were or even as they are right now. Things are accelerating and picking up speed. The days of ease and comfort are gone. There will be great persecution and tribulation on every hand. Men's hearts will fail them for fear. There will be distress — distress of nations.

The things you hold dear, the things you hold so tightly to

now, the things you expend all your effort on, the things you crave and desire, the things that seem so important now, will all be worthless in the light of what is happening around you. They hold no eternal value and bear the fruit of nothingness. Your heart will grieve as you realize that you gave yourself to things — things of this world — and haphazardly planted My Word and at random dug for My hidden treasure and sought for Me at your convenience. You were not willing to sell all. You were not willing to die to self. Your flesh rules!

Come to Me, My children, come. Listen. Heed My call; listen to My voice. Lay it all down now. Die to it all so that you can be raised up in newness of life and become My salt and My light to a dying world. The only way you can become salt and light is by letting go, laying it all down, dying to self.

The Storm Clouds Gather

Because My people have looked to man and elevated man and followed man, I will remove from their midst those whom their souls have desired. I will bring them into a desert. I will bring them into a wilderness, a dry and barren place where there is no water except Mine, a place where there is no bread except Mine. They will have to dig for water and search for My bread in order to live and be sustained. I will strip them of all fleshly props and programs. I will reveal to them the emptiness of following after man and man's ways. I will show them the sinfulness of their own ways. I will bring them into the wilderness to try them and test them until they see that the desire of their heart has not been to seek and know Me but to walk in their own ways and satisfy their own lusts and desires. They shall cry out to Me in despair when they recognize how their hearts have followed after man to satisfy the cravings and desires of their own flesh.

And they know Me not. And they hear not My call to

come and meet Me daily in a place of love — to eat and drink and sup and fellowship and prepare their hearts to be My bride. Oh, My people are far from Me. The days grow dark. The storm clouds gather. The time is drawing near when I shall come for My bride — My prepared bride, My cleansed and purified bride, My bride who has a single eye and a heart devoted to Me and seeking only Me. But they hear not My call to prepare. They hear not My call to come for daily cleansing. They refuse to come. Their hearts are set on other things — how they may please themselves and satisfy their fleshly appetites and desires.

Oh, that My people had a heart for Me. Oh, that they would turn and come to Me and prepare their hearts to be My bride. The hour is late, the time is short. Answer the call, My people. Come, come out from among them and seek Me — the Lord your God, your Lover and Friend — with all of your heart!

Judgment, Persecution, and Purification[2]

The Lord says: Hear My word. The time that has been marked by My blessings and gifts is being replaced now by My judgment and purification. What I have not accomplished by blessings and gifts, I will accomplish by judgment and purification. My people (My Church) are desperately in need of this judgment. They have continued in an adulterous relationship with the spirit of the world. They are not only infected with sin, they teach sin, pamper sin, embrace sin, and dismiss sin. Leadership is unable to handle it — fragmentation, confusion throughout the ranks. Satan goes where he will and infects whom he will. He has free access throughout My people; I will not stand for this.

My people are more under the spirit of the world than they are under the Spirit of My baptism. [Their actions] are more determined by fear of what others will think of them —fear of failure and rejection in the world, loss of respect by neighbors and superiors and those around them—than they are determined by fear of Me and fear of infidelity to My Word. Therefore your situation is very, very weak; your power is limited. You cannot be considered, at this point, in the center of the battle and the conflict that is going on.

So the time has now come on all of you — a time of judgment and purification. Sin will be called sin. Satan will be unmasked. Fidelity will be held up for what it is and should be. My faithful servants will be seen and come together. They will not be many in number. It will be a difficult and necessary time. There will be collapse, difficulties throughout the world; but more to the issue — there will be persecution and purification among My people! You will have to stand for what you believe. You will have to choose between the world and Me! You will have to choose what word you will follow and whom you will respect. In that choice, what has not been accomplished by the time of blessings and gifts will be accomplished. What has not been accomplished in the baptism and the flooding of the gifts of My Spirit will be accomplished in a baptism of fire!

The fire will move among you and will burn up what is chaff. The fire will move among you, individually and corporately, around the world. I will not tolerate the situation that is going on. I will not tolerate the mixture and adulterous treating of gifts, graces, and blessing, with infidelity, sin, and prostitution! My time is now among you. What you need to do is come before Me in total submission to My plan. In the total submission of this hour, you need to drop things that are your own, the things of the past.

What you need to do is see yourselves, and those you have responsibility for, in the light of this hour of judgment and purification. You need to see them in that way and do for them what will best help them to stand strong and be among My faithful servants. For there will be casualties. It will not be easy, but it is necessary. It is necessary that My people be in fact My people, that My Church be in fact My Church, and that My Spirit in fact bring forth purity of life, purity and fidelity to the Gospel.

God's Warning to the Church

There is a wake-up call sounding forth to the Church in this hour: Wake up! Wake up! Arouse yourself. Get up. Shake yourselves. It is time to awake and prepare yourselves. Put down and put away the food and delicacies of this world. You have eaten and partaken with the world and have become drunken and unable to stand. You reel like a drunken man! You fall and drop into a deep slumber and know not that My judgments are even now upon this land.

They come with a swiftness. They come like pangs upon a woman in travail. Wake up, wake up, My people! Don't you hear the rumblings? For even the very earth cries out in pain to be delivered. And what will you do in that day when your delicacies have vanished and your comforts and pacifiers are no more?

Oh, do you not hear the call of the Spirit? Awake! Awake! Prepare! Seek Me with all of your heart. You trust in your riches. You trust in your finances. You trust in your outward display of love for Me. But I look on the heart, and I call for repentance and purging of the inward parts, the secret parts. My call is for all of the heart and a seeking of Me first — above all things. All else will put you in a deep sleep, a deep slumber; and you will not know that the day is, even now, upon you.

In mercy I call. Turn, turn with all of your hearts, or you will not be ready! You will be unprepared for the judgments that are now upon the Church. In mercy I hold back severity.

24

In mercy I call. Oh, do not be complacent and dull of hearing. Wake up and heed My warning. The day cometh very swiftly!

MAKE LAMENTATION. MAKE LAMENTATION. Cry out; hold not back! Repent and turn, that you may be spared the judgment. In mercy I call.

The Wrath of God[3]

"Thou, even Thou, art to be feared: and who may stand in Thy sight when once Thou art angry?" (Psalm 76:7)

As the dispensation of grace is drawing to a close, there shall be a beginning of the unleashing of My wrath upon the wicked of the world such as there has not been since the days of Noah! It shall be equal to the great grace which I have shown the world.

For two thousand years My anger and My judgments upon the wicked have been held back because of the dispensation of grace and the covenant agreement I have made with My Son. But as the days of the Gentiles are drawing to a close, so also are the days of grace quickly passing away, and the world shall see an unleashing of My fury such as these generations have never known. It will be a time of astonishment and woe, woe, woe!

I am not blind to the sins which the ungodly are committing and flaunting in My face. But My wrath and fury have been held back until the days of grace are finished. Now I declare that they are almost over, and in the closing down of the days of grace you are seeing only the beginning of My wrath, but it shall increase. . . .

This is the beginning of sorrows. Prepare your hearts, My beloved, to see an outpouring of My wrath, for it shall begin **BEFORE** the catching away of My bride. Yea, it has already begun. The plagues have begun. Run through the camp and warn the people, and "Let no man deceive you with vain words: for because of these things cometh the wrath of God upon the children of disobedience. Be not ye therefore partakers with them." [Ephesians 5:6,7]

Hard Times Are Coming[4]

Hard times are coming soon, very soon. Prepare now. Prepare!

I have been calling you to a deeper and closer walk with Me, to put aside time to spend with Me; and still you neglect that time. You go through your days without spending time in My Word, time in prayer and in your secret prayer closets. Unless you put aside that time with Me daily and really get to know Me, in these Last Days you will not be able to stand.

My children, I love you very much and long for you to spend time with Me — to know Me as never before. Many of My children are walking in defeat and are allowing the things of this world, rather than the things of Me, to consume them. I would say to you: Walk in My Spirit, live by My Spirit, and spend time with Me in My Word and in your secret prayer closets. Then you will be able to stand in the storms of time and in all that is about to happen on the face of this whole earth. Put aside all other presumptions and plans, and seek Me for your daily provision. Allow Me to be that provision for you.

Terrible Times Are On Their Way

My people, hear! Hear! You who have ears to hear, seek My Spirit to lift you up. Be lifted up in the Spirit, and ask Me to show you your condition, My people, as it really is! Come up with Me and see as I see. My people argue and fight and compete with one another, just like those who do not know Me. Did you not come to Me on the day of your Salvation to learn truth? You yearned to know the God of all truth. I have offered you freely the Living Water from My well of Salvation. You turn away and drink of the filthy water of the world's cistern. You sin in your love of the gods and goddesses of this world. You want to choose once again to believe lies.

Hard times are, like the tide, coming in. They lap closer and closer, inch by inch, toward your feet. You think you will never be found out; you think your heart is not hardened; you think your conscience still works. Oh, how blind you have become! You have returned to the blind state you were born in, and you do not even know it!

Have you not seen? Have you not heard in the Wind of the Spirit? Disaster is coming closer to you! How foolish My people are! Disaster is in the winds, in the floods. And to think, My people, this is only the beginning!

Oh, how I have loved you with never-ending love ever since Adam and Eve were created. I have loved and yearned and taught and trained and blessed you with meat and drink, with vegetables and oil and large herds and flocks and safe dwellings and health. I have wooed you and declared all My intentions to you. I have covenanted with you through the Blood of My Son and asked nothing but that you LOVE Me with all your heart, soul, mind, and strength, and your neighbor as yourself. I have promised you hundreds of blessings and safety and many healthy children and peace in the nation, peace in Israel. But, do you love Me? Do you teach your children all about Me? Do you bring My good news to your neighbors around this earth?

I must punish My children — as late as I can possibly make it — who do not love Me, but love and worship their idols. Sin is rampant in My earth! Terrible hard times are on their way to this earth! Seek Me, and I will come to you and lift your spirit high above these hard times.

During the Holocaust[5]

In the coming holocaust, I will again be establishing "cities of refuge," as it were, for the safety of those I know and those who have taken the time to know Me. These spiritual "cities" will be havens of rest, provision, and safety for My bride for the season of change before My return. Unseen walls of protection, holy nourishment, and sweet refreshing will be available to those who have learned to feed on the Source of real life. My Holy Spirit will guide My chosen children to these places in times of need.

Do not limit Me by your carnal understanding as to the nature of what I am saying. Go to My Word: I have confused the enemies of My people that they might escape. I have blinded the eyes of aggressors so "paths" of safety could be seen. I have opened the eyes of My people to heavenly warriors, that they might see alliances stronger than foes.

Nothing is too hard for Me. Safety is not where you are, but who you are with. When you are truly with Me, nothing or no one can touch what I call sacred. Come to Me. I am your place of safety, your ever present city of refuge forevermore.

Who Can Endure God's Fierce Anger?[6]

Who can withstand My indignation? Who can endure My fierce anger? Though I am a refuge in times of trouble, I am about to pour out My wrath on those in disobedience to Me. My flood is about to become a torrent to those who have chosen not to listen. The crevices in the rocks that hide you are the pathways of the rushing waters I will use to purify My people. You will be washed away if your stronghold is not chosen by Me.

Come to safety. Come to Me. Rid yourselves of your adultery; the time is past for it to go unnoticed. Your shame will be exposed for what it really is: works of the flesh. My ways are the only way. Walk in them.

Many Christians Will Fall[7]

Many are those who sit neglectful, loving the world and the things of the world. Many seek the life of the earth, but they do not prepare themselves to meet the Holy One. Jesus is coming! Do not be lazy!

Terror and great pain is coming upon the earth! The devil will take upon himself power, and he will attempt to make war with the holy. But Christ, the Victorious One, will come and will save His people.

Proud men! — all those who pretend to be teachers, and never living the life; all those who say they worship Me, yet their hearts are far from Me. Says the Lord: I will make them part of the suffering, torment, and terror, that they may call upon Me, but I will not answer.

Those that today humble themselves and seek Me with a clean heart, in that day — the hard day — will be glad and will rejoice. The power of the devil will increase greatly in this country [America], and many Christians will fall in its chains because they have dishonored Me with their lives — in their pride, their arrogance, and their vanity — thinking they are holy and are worshipping Me, yet *never really worshipping Me.*

The winds and the storms that will begin against the Christians in this country will take many. **Those who remain standing will be very few!** Humble yourselves. Be holy. Seek Me more than ever, kneeling before Me often, that in the hard days I may save you, says the Lord.

The End of Things

It is the end of things as you see them now, the end of things as they were before. I am shutting down, closing down, taking away. That which once seemed fruitful, active, and growing, I am bringing to nothing. Sometimes I am just moving and rearranging. Sometimes I am scattering. This is My last-day working. My remnant will go through a deep purging, a violent shaking, and intense heat — in the form of trials — to test and prove, to prepare and cleanse, to sanctify and set apart. Think it not strange . . . I am testing your hearts. Where is your heart? What is it set on?

Judgment Comes Swiftly!

The morning cometh, but also the night. Do not trust in the things you can now see. Do not be deceived by the things you can see in the light now, for the night cometh. The night cometh, the darkness of the night. Men grope in the darkness; they stumble and fall. They fear, they panic. The security of the day will suddenly pass away!

Those who are not watching and preparing will think it is only a happenstance, at first — something that will pass, an inconvenience. They will not recognize that it is from My hand, that I am beginning to pour out My judgments on a Church that will not turn and come to Me with all of their hearts. I've called and called and waited and warned and held back. My heart is grieved. They go on in their own ways and heed not My warnings.

Watch now, what of the night? What of the night? It cometh. Declare what thou seest. The judgment comes swiftly!

When the Devastation Begins

As time as you know it draws to a close, things around you will accelerate. It is imperative that you come away to the secret place right now — that quiet, peaceful place of love. I resorted there often. Go to it often. Leave the hustle and bustle and hurry and clamor around you, and hide in the "secret place of the stairs" [see Song of Solomon 2:14]. Seek it out; desire it; yearn for it now. Familiarize yourself with it now, **or you won't know how or where to find it when the devastation begins.**

3. Where the Church and God's People are at the Present Time

A. An Overview

Disease in the Church

My Church is being destroyed from within. And My people within the Church are being eaten alive, as it were, by a disease called "sin." This disease is the result of spiritual harlotry, spiritual adultery. I have stood many times in My Church next to My beloved ones and have pleaded with them to come, to come away with Me to the secret place, to come home to Me, to come to be loved and cherished by Me, to come to be directed and corrected and comforted and married to Me; but they have refused. They have smiled; they have patted Me on the shoulder, as it were, kissed Me on the cheek, said, "I love you" and have gone off to do their own thing. They have gone off to their other loves — their other loves!

As a result of their sin and waywardness, the Church is sick — sick and dying. It is dying from within, from the very inward parts of the Church. My people are dying because the heart is diseased and the heart is broken. The heart is actually cut in two and divided; and I have so small a portion of the heart of My Church at this time. For the Church is enamored with her other loves. My people seek them, they follow them, they delight in them; and they hear not My call. They hardly hear Me anymore, calling and calling, calling them to come, to come away.

And it is the time, it is the time to come away. It's the time of the singing of the birds. It's a time of love, the time of love as the bride prepares.

On the one hand, there are those who are hearing My call and responding to My call of love, responding to the cleansing process that is taking place for the preparation of the bride. They are responding. But on the other hand, the Church and My people are not hearing the call. The call seems too harsh. The call seems too hard. The call seems too demanding. Surely, surely, they think, they need to be comforted in all of their grievances and all of their hurts; and all of their appetites need to be fed. . . . And they are not responding to My call at this time.

But I continue to call. I continue to woo My Church. I continue to call them. I want to heal them. I want to make them perfectly whole. But they are not hearing. They are off in a frenzy of activities. And a flurry of gaiety surrounds them as they whirl and they twirl, as it were, and as they dance to another song, another tune; and they hear not My call. They hear not the song of the Lover. They hear not His call. It has been covered over because of the loudness and the blasting of the other things that are calling out to them.

Oh, oh, I call, I call, and I call! I want My bride prepared. I want those whom I have called and chosen, to come to Me. But they have chosen another way, and it is the path of destruction. It is the path of death! But they heed not My call. They heed it not! And My fire which is even now burning out the dross in My bride, burning out those things that are not right, will soon be turned in wrath and fury and anger on those who have not heeded My call. But they have defiled themselves and have become a part of the world and the world system.

I, the Lord your God, call in love and in mercy. Come, come to Me. Come and be purified, so that I can call you and look upon you as My undefiled one.

A Den of Thieves

Just as I cleansed My house at the beginning and end of My earthly ministry, so will I also cleanse My house before I return for My bride. There will be a time of deep purging, cleansing, and purifying by My Spirit. I will judge My house by righteous judgment. It will be by and according to My mercy. I will sweep it clean.

There is much that has been brought in, in My Name, that is not of Me. My house shall be called a House of Prayer for all people, but you have made it a den of thieves! You have robbed My house of its very name. You buy, but not of Me. You sell that which is lame and inferior and have made My House a house of merchandise.

It is not according to My standard. It is not according to My rule. I am not high and lifted up in your sanctuary. You have lifted up the things your hearts and flesh desire, and have ignored the true call of the Spirit to make My house a House of Prayer. It is what I, the Lord your God, have called My house, but you have sought out other things and ignored the way of the Cross and have not denied yourself. My heart grieves over a people who want to be called by My Name but refuse to be identified with Me in My true ministry and desire.

How long can I stand a dirty house? It reeks of flesh — flesh is on display, flesh is in control! As long as you continue to please your flesh and the desire of men, then it is not My House. For My house shall be called a House of Prayer for all people.

Many Ministries Are Defiled

Many ministries are defiled. They seek to elevate themselves and please the people. The people gather to receive, more than to give unto Me. The people are looking for words to heal and comfort. They want to be called out and zeroed in on and told their answers. It is centered on this many times.

And the people are not content to meet with Me and come and savor My Word and mull over My Word and be penetrated and divided by My Word and cleansed and corrected by My Word. Always the people are looking for the supernatural. If a lowly, quiet servant of Mine comes into their midst and gently gives and divides the piercing Word of Truth to lay hearts open and bare before Me, they are labeled dull and unappealing.

I will not move through a self-seeking, selfish, self-centered vessel! I will use the meek, humble, broken servant, wanting and desiring Me, willing to proclaim My Name regardless of popular opinion or demands. This defilement is a grievance unto Me and a stench in My nostrils!

A Word for Pastors[8]

Where are My Jeremiahs? Where are My faithful servants whom I have called forth to serve My people in humility? Where are My prophets whom I have called to sound the trumpet to warn the people in the hour of destruction? Where are My watchmen on the walls? Why will ye not sound the trumpet when you see the enemy approaching? [see Ezekiel 33:6-9]

Has the spirit of slumber fallen upon you? Have you made a covenant of silence with those who refuse to warn My people, lest you lose their respect and honor? Whose honor do you seek? Is it the honor of a fallen race? Or is it the honor of the saints of all ages who were faithful? — who spoke truth, who warned of sin and judgment to come, who died as martyrs.

Are you afraid of dying for Me? Are you afraid of being accused of madness and error by those whose vain respect you have gained? You say, "I will not be an alarmist. I will not frighten the people. It will cause panic if I speak the truth. Some will get angry. I will lose my congregation! I will lose my pulpit! I will lose my salary."

I say unto you: What is a pulpit? It is nothing but a piece of furniture if the man behind it does not preach My present-day truth — even the message that the Holy Spirit wants him to give for this day and this hour.

What is a congregation? It is only a gathering of people who are unprepared and inefficient in an hour of crisis, if the true Word has not been preached to them. It is even a blind people who will not know which way to go when the End-Time crises come upon them suddenly.

What is a church building? It is only a house of back-sliders who play at religion if they are not warned to repent, forsake their sins, and flee from the wrath to come!

What is a pastor? Is he a true shepherd of My flock? Or is he a hireling? He must be faithful to warn My sheep and to correct them and to punish them, with strong words of warning. He must lay the rod of My Word across their stubborn necks; for My people will go astray as long as you permit them to do so.

There is sin in My Church — gross sin! They bring into My House the earnings of their sin — even the hire of a harlot. [see Micah 1:7] And My pastors accept it and are glad for it. . . .

The hour of sorrows has come. [see Matthew 24:8] It is

even the hour of My wrath! But My pastors refuse to warn My people. There is a spirit of compromise on them!

They promise mercy to those who deserve no mercy. "For if you sin wilfully after that we have received the knowledge of the truth, there remaineth no more sacrifice for sins, but a certain fearful looking for of judgment and fiery indignation, which shall devour the adversaries. [For even] he that despised Moses' law died without mercy . . . Of how much sorer punishment, suppose ye, shall he be thought worthy, who hath trodden under foot the Son of God, and hath counted the Blood of the covenant — wherewith he was sanctified — an unholy thing, and hath done despite unto the Spirit of grace? For we know Him that hath said, Vengeance belongeth unto Me; I will recompense, saith the Lord. And again, The Lord shall judge His people." [see Hebrews 10:26-30]

The pastors preach a message of "unsanctified mercy." They promise peace when there is rioting and death on their streets. They promise peace when the enemy bombs their Trade Centers, and their homes are full of fighting. They promise blessing when their homes and places of business are collapsing in earthquakes, and fires are raging in their suburbs and destroying their homes, and their farms are inundated with the floods of many waters.

The rivers overflow because the heavens weep. The fires are lit by madmen whose souls have not found the true Prince of Peace. There is no peace! And there will be no peace as long as there is no peace for the unborn baby who lies in the womb of his mother. All who promise peace, blessing, and prosperity speak a lie!

IT IS A TIME TO WEEP! Call out the mourning women and let them make haste and take up a wailing for us that our eyes may run down with tears, and our eyelids gush out with waters. Let the voice of wailing be heard out of Zion, for we are ravaged; we are greatly ashamed of the sin in the land. [see Jeremiah 9:17-25]

Hear the mothers weeping for their young sons shot dead in the streets of our cities. Hear them weeping and angry for their little daughters who are pregnant. Hear the forsaken wives who have been left desolate by their unfaithful husbands and lovers, men controlled by demons of lust.

Go to your morgues and count the bodies of your teenagers who have died of drugs. Then, count the dollars of the abortionists; see their summer homes, their yachts, their condominiums. See the palaces that gambling has purchased with money "stolen" from foolish people who are controlled by greed and the spirit of chance. See the corruption in government — the misuse of money, of power, and of words (by false promises) — and know the end of all this is come up before Me. .

I will not be mocked any longer! I will not allow them to challenge Me any longer! I will not allow them to defy Me to My face any longer! I will show this world one more time — like I did in the days of Noah — that I am God! And nothing will be the same anymore. It will not be "business as usual."

I am, even now, marking those who sigh and cry for the abomination that is done in the midst of My people. And the slaughter weapon is even now in the hands of the destroying angels! [see Ezekiel 9:1-11]

Warn your people, My pastors. For if you refuse to sound the warning, their blood — even the blood of the aborted babies, the blood of the drug addicts, the blood of those who will die of euthanasia, the blood of the suicide victims, the blood of the children who are shot to death on your streets, and the blood of those who die and will continue to die in the coming calamities — will ALL be upon your hands! [see Ezekiel 3:16-21]

A Partying Spirit

There is a partying spirit in the land and in the Church. It is an "eat, drink, and be merry" spirit. It is the same spirit Moses encountered when he came down from the mountain after being shut in with God. It is the same spirit that is recorded in Matthew 24. The heart of the evil and unwise servant said, "My Lord delayeth His coming," and he began to eat and drink with the drunken. It is a partying spirit. It is a heart going after the things of this world. It is a heart refusing to hear and respond to the call of the Spirit to watch and prepare and be ready.

Lay down the things of this world, and lay up in your heart and soul My true riches and My true treasures. But you must lay down the one in order to take up and lay up the other. Do not be deceived. I will not be mocked. That which you sow is what you will reap. If you sow to the flesh, you will reap corruption. If you sow to the Spirit, you will reap life everlasting. Lay down the things of this world. Run from this partying spirit. If you refuse, you will not be ready for My soon return.

You Have Enthroned Self

You, as My children, surround yourselves with ease and comforts. Your cares and concerns are really not for people, their needs and burdens and distresses, for you care only for yourselves. The main concern of your day, everyday, has been centered wholly on your needs, burdens, loves, and desires. You fit Me in where it is convenient for you. You are so busy fighting the battle of self and things, that you hardly notice the lost, the hurting, the hungry — be they in the Church or in the world. And you say you love Me and you desire to do My works, but only in your own way and time and according to your own will.

39

How blind you are, how rich in the things of this world. You continually strive to get to the place of doing service for Me, but you are like the Israelites wandering in the wilderness. Their goal was the Promised Land, but their hearts were set on other things. They loved the world and the things of this world. The fruit of that love was death and separation! They never made it into the Promised Land. So near, yet so far.

You need, My children, to evaluate where you are and where it is you are going. What is your heart set on? What is it that you want? I am looking for a people willing to do My will — My way. I am looking for a people who will willingly cut ties to their worldly, self-seeking, self-desiring, self-righteous acts, deeds, and loves. You have enthroned self! How far you are from lowliness of spirit and a mercying heart.

Oh, how My heart grieves. In your blindness you do not see it, and you continue to surround yourselves with your ease and comforts as My heart cries out for those who will strip themselves of all covetousness so that they can stand before Me in prayer and intercession with a pure heart and clean hands. Look around you; take an inventory. Listen. What is your heart set on? How much is enough? Let Me do this stripping work in your life My way. Lay everything down. I will give you what you need, when you need it and how you need it. Lay down your preconceived ideas along with your human reasonings. Let Me, the Master Potter, shape and mold you into a vessel fit for My use.

Death and Separation

How long, how long, how long will My people go on in their own ways? They seek Me not, neither do they know Me. Their hearts are filled with surfeiting and drunkenness. They seek their own pleasure and do their own will. They hear not My voice calling and calling and calling to them to come and to seek Me with their whole heart. How long will they go on in their ways? How long will they refuse to turn from their wicked and sinful ways? They hear Me not. The end result will be death and separation!

A Commentary[9]*

by Ron Auch

Finally the question can be settled once and for all concerning the Rapture of the Church. I will share with you the revelation God gave me regarding this issue.

Since the time Jesus left the earth, there have been different views as to when the Rapture was going to take place. You can find someone that subscribes to your view, whether it is pre-trib, mid-trib, post-trib, or even "pan-trib." The pan-trib theory is that of not claiming to know anything other than, in the end, it will all pan out. There are those who do not believe in a Rapture at all, and those who believe in multiple Raptures.

Now the question can finally be settled. It's as simple as this: No matter which theory you hold to, it doesn't matter, because THE CHURCH IN AMERICA IS GOING TO MISS IT — no matter when it happens!**

Who are we kidding? We can't even fool the world anymore. They look at us from their worldly eyes and know we are no different than they are.

41

We have lost a knowledge of the Holy; we can't discern the difference between the holy and profane. When we go to church, we aren't sure if we should sing a hymn, or rap, or rock and roll. Our "prophets" are so fearful of losing their offerings, they won't deal with the sin in the Church. We are in a big mess, and, to top it all off, we can't call the Church to prayer! She is not interested in spiritual things and yet foolishly believes she is ready for the return of Jesus Christ!

We read about the Parable of the Ten Virgins and think that the five foolish ones must be someone else. We don't even have the basic characteristic of a bride in waiting: a longing for the groom. The next time you hear a prophecy "expert" tell you about when the Rapture is going to happen, will you have to say, "It isn't going to happen for me; I belong to the Church that is rich and in need of nothing"?

["Because you say, 'I am rich, have become wealthy, and have need of nothing' — and do not know that you are wretched, miserable, poor, blind, and naked — I counsel you to buy from Me gold refined in the fire, that you may be rich; and white garments, that you may be clothed, that the shame of your nakedness may not be revealed; and anoint your eyes with eye salve, that you may see. As many as I love, I rebuke and chasten. Therefore, be zealous and repent." (Revelation 3:17-19 NKJ)]

*Edited version of a previously published article.

**Editor's note: the Church as it is now.

Come Out of the Harlot Church[10]

"And I heard another voice from Heaven, saying, Come out of her, My people, that ye be not partakers of her sins, and that ye receive not of her plagues." (Revelation 18:4)

I hate the religious facade of the world's Babylonian system. "Having a form of godliness, but denying the power thereof" is what I see as I pass through your Sunday morning congregations.

To the world's observer it appears to be a gathering of dedicated, sincere, God-loving people who have come to worship Me. But sad to say, this is not the case. Instead, My house has become a habitation of devils, the hold of every foul spirit, the cage of every unclean and hateful bird.

In all nations where My Church has spread, carried by My dedicated missionaries, I have seen the corrupting of My bride, My Church — the salt of the earth — into a house of thieves, a habitation of devils, a lurking place for every foul spirit, and a cage for every hateful bird.

There is no way, when it has become that corrupt, to convert or change her. The only thing left is to come out of her, separate yourself from her. A split is better than the defilement of the lot; the cutting off of a right arm is better than the poisoning of the blood stream. Cry mightily unto Me for cleansing in My house; for judgment is surely coming! The angel is come down from Heaven, having great power, and as the earth is being enlightened with His glory, every evil shall be detected. Nothing shall be hidden. Nothing shall be made to appear what it isn't.

Do not cling to that which I will destroy. For the judgment shall be sudden, and it shall be great, and it shall be swift, even in one hour!

3. Where the Church and God's People are at the Present Time

B. Things

The Things of This World

The cares of this world are overtaking you. Sow to the flesh, and of the flesh ye shall reap corruption. Sow to the Spirit, and of the Spirit ye shall reap life everlasting. [see Galatians 6:8] "To be carnally minded is death; but to be spiritually minded is life and peace." [Romans 8:6]

Oh My child, be not overcome with the things of this world. Set your affections on Me, not on the things of this world, not on the things that do not satisfy, not on temporal things, not on things that are passing, that the enemy can break through and steal. For where your treasure is, there will your heart be also. Set your affections on things above. Be seated with Me in heavenly places. Seek Me with all of your heart. Desire Me more than anyone or anything. Seek Me first, and all these other things will be added unto you.

How quickly the glitter and sparkle of earthly things fade. They are wood, hay, and stubble. They have no eternal value. Your meat is to do the will of your Father. Nothing else satisfies. I give you water that you will never thirst again and bread that you will not hunger. Oh, be not satisfied with the weak and beggarly elements of this world, for the things of this world shall pass away, but My Word shall stand forever. Feed on Me!

Things and Self

All the things you hold on to so tightly and preserve and protect will someday be someone else's. You guard and protect and preserve to the point of esteeming your things above people and overlook a bleeding heart and a sorrowful spirit. You preserve yourself and your things unto yourself. Do not hold on so tightly. Esteem them lightly. Keep as your most treasured possession My love for you, and My Word; and walk in love, godly fear, and obedience.

I have shown you that the word "die" is in obedience. Die to your things and your desires, wants, and cravings; and come to Me with all your heart. Come and follow Me. I will teach and show you how to live and order your days and your life. I will help you sift and sort through your things so that you'll be free to be low, and flow in My mercy love. This is what you have asked for and desired to do. There is only one way: it is the way of the Cross. There is only one way to intimacy: forsaking all else and running and pursuing Me with all of your heart. All! I ask for ALL — all your love, all your fear, all your obedience.

Surrender All

[The person who received the prophecy speaking]: "As we look on our things, our wants, and our desires, and mind earthly things, we're not aware that there are people whose bodies are suffering in sickness and pain. Their thoughts are no longer on things. The care and possession of things has faded far into the background, and they hold no appeal or desire for them. Their main concern is their battle against sickness. For those of us who are not sick or in pain, how long will we mind earthly things to the extent that we are giving ourselves to these things? — charting and planning and deciding our own course, as it were, still in charge of our days, thoughts, desires, plans, and will."

[God speaking]: All things will not be as you supposed. The main order of your day, in any circumstance, should be to draw close to Me and to listen and obey. I will lead, guide, and direct you. You make simple things so complicated. You surround yourself with the fruit of your natural reasoning mind and don't even give Me a chance.

Abandon yourself to Me. Surrender all. All! You are still at the center of your will, for as long as you control and decide, it's your will. You don't give Me a chance. You have set a standard, and you are convinced and determined that that is what you need. If you pursue it, I will give it to you, but there is a leanness that comes with it. It will not be the portion I have for you. You are struggling and kicking against the pricks. I will use the simple things of this world to confound the wise of this world.

Come, learn of Me. I am meek and lowly of heart. Come, empty yourself of all things, and let Me fill you with Myself.

3. Where the Church and God's People are at the Present Time

C. Works of the Flesh

Works of the Flesh[11]

"In the Name of the Lord," you say. You go about your business doing your works and call them Mine. How can what you do be truly Mine if you don't spend enough time with Me to hear Me, to search My heart, to find My ways, to know Me? I am not in your feasts. I am not in your programs. I am not in your fellowships. A time is coming when those who think they hear My voice will see and understand who they have really been listening to. It is not Me. All the works of the flesh will wash away as so much grime. I will not complete what I did not initiate.

Stop praying for things. Stop working for men and their desires. Begin praying to search Me out. I can be found. I desire to be found. Those who choose to know Me are wise. Those who come to Me will walk the straight, safe path. My ways are sure. My time is well spent for those who have heard Me.

I am not interested in your works. All that you do in the flesh is soon to blow away as chaff in the harvester's field. Only the pure wheat from the fine seed will be used to feed the multitude.

When will you come to Me? What will it take to bring your heart to the place where I can use it? Don't you see? Have you become so hardened to My voice that I can no longer move you?

My will for you is purity of spirit, mind, and motive. My place for you is with Me. When will you come? When will you choose the quiet with Me over the din of activity? What will it take to bend your knees, still your heart, and receive My presence?

Turn now to Me. Doing good for Me instead of coming to Me achieves nothing. Stop. Listen. Come. I am waiting.

I call you to holiness, but you are too busy to spend time with Me. I call you to a crucified life, but you cannot die to yourself. I call you to present My Son to those who are dead that they might receive His life, but you curse them in My presence.

Can you not see how cold you really are? Can you not see how far you've strayed from My purposes for your life? Who are you saving by your actions? What are the purposes of your comings and goings? Whose agenda are you following and what is its end?

Wake up! The harvest is white and the workers are few. Pray to the Lord of the Harvest. What are His purposes? What is His agenda? Pray for wisdom that you might see with His eyes and move with His heart. The time is short and much is to be done.

The harvest is white right now, but My Church is so busy doing "good" things that they can't see My things to do! I ask you, *when did My Gospel call you to any activity that did not have the eternity of the souls of men and women as its purpose?* When did I ever ask you to protect your rights? Where in My Word does it say that you must occupy your time doing works that have no impact on the Salvation of your enemies? I am not in the midst of your projects of men! The ultimate purpose of these doctrines of men is the preservation of your freedoms, your way. I have set you free My way, so that you might share My Light in the darkest places for the good of those in bondage. How pitiful and powerless your works are!

You have chosen this day whom you will serve. All projects that have fleshly motives will fail. I call them wood, hay, and stubble, about to be burned away. Some of you will stand empty-handed before Me on that day. You think that your arms are full to present offerings to Me. They are barren and of no eternal worth.

Turn to Me. Remember My desires. I care about the souls of those that are perishing. You care about preserving your life and call it My desire for you. It is not Me you are listening to. Turn now to My purposes.

I have sent My Son, Jesus Christ, to die; and I have raised Him from the dead that the world might again be brought into fellowship with Me. I have sent My Holy Spirit to indwell each one that might believe and submit wholly to Him. He is to exhibit to a world, dying and out of real answers, the only answer — the life of Jesus — and it is to be done through those who believe. By His life in you, the believer, others are to see how Jesus loved, lived, and died, so they might not perish. Your life is to be so empowered by My Holy Spirit that the blind might look at it and recognize the life of Jesus and be brought to Him for their Salvation.

Instead of them seeing Who My Son really is, they see

weak, pitiful, empty ramblings of moral finger-pointing and self-righteous, self-serving religious bigotry! The Name of My glorious Son has been brought to such low esteem in the eyes of your world because of your cold, fruitless religion, that they laugh and mock Him, instead of calling Him Lord.

When will you hear what I have been telling you? When will you stop your foolish, powerless activity and lock yourself up with Me that you might really exhibit the life of My Son, empowered by My Holy Spirit? Repent, turn, stop — now! I am waiting for you.

How many people have seen My Son in your life? How many have chosen to serve Me through My Son because they have seen Him in you? *How many have turned from their ways to My ways because of your ways?* Does your neighbor know that you are My tabernacle? Does your enemy know that you are told to lay your life down for him and have agreed to do so?

Do you know that I love the abortionist, the pornographer, the homosexual? Do you know that I have sent you to them that they might see My Son through you, that they might accept Him? Do you have the eternity of your every contact in mind when you address them? If not, why not?

As My people go about their own version of what My Word says, I, the Lord God, am used as a license for them to remain in their sin, or I am left out completely. Where in My Word does it say that My people are to be political or moral watchdogs? Where in My Word does it say that My people are to condemn the sinner? Where in My Word does it say that My people are to search out those things that give them comfort?

I have called My people to holiness. I have called My people to be set apart from all that resembles the world. I sent My Son that the dead may be given life. All do not receive that life. They choose to remain dead.

Your flurry of activities, your agenda of issue involvement, your moral judgment and all of its associated activities, have not and cannot bring [life to] those who choose to remain dead. *I am not in your outcry against your world. I am only in your outcry for mercy for your hardened heart.*

Repent and turn now. See your spiritual adultery. See your hardened hearts. See your dead, cold churches and weep for them. I have called you to tell the blind of a way that they might see My Son, Jesus Christ. Why do you insist on doing your own will rather than submitting to Me to have your heart changed, that they might see Jesus in you?

Early Morning Conversation[12]

"Yes, Lord?"

The last call is coming to My people. I call and no one hears. Hope for the lost is nonexistent in the minds of the dry remnant. Caring for My desires is nonexistent in those whom I have entrusted with My Word. Fear of Me is far from the minds of those who consume My grace on their sinful lives.

No more! I am the Almighty God. Repent! Return to your "first love," My people. You are cold. You are empty. **You are trying to replace My presence with the works that make you feel worthy.** Those works only serve your inner fears and needs, not My purposes. Repent. Return to your first love. Seek Me and live.

"But how do I start, Lord?"

51

Adjust your timetable to fall in line with Mine, and you will be free. Your struggles, worries, and concerns do not have a place in the life I have chosen for you.

Think on this: I am God — the one true God. I have all power — power far beyond your most intense imagination. You are My child through your acceptance of My Son Jesus and what He has done for you. Because of that, My life would freely flow to you if you would choose to accept it. That would mean that nothing could harm the eternal you. You could be free from all strife and worry simply by trusting that I care enough to take care of you. [But] your life is *not* free — only because you hinder Me. Satan is defeated. There is no hold over your life to stop you from receiving My presence. Why do you choose to believe the lies of the world that bind and condemn you, instead of My Word that eternally works in you to set you free?

I love you. Choose to receive Me and My Word, and you will be free.

"But Lord, I am so weak. I have failed You so often."

My holding power is much more powerful than the sinning power of your flesh. When will you grasp the reality of what has been done on the Cross for you? Its work runs deeper than any force. Its power is so much greater than anything that may attempt to come against it.

When Jesus died, all that hindered My presence from becoming active and available in your life was removed forever. When He arose, death itself was defeated. Think on that. What that means for you is the freedom to receive My life, My eternal life, and the wealth that comes to you by My presence being with you in your life forever.

When hardship comes, don't attempt to deal with it by your knowledge or ability. Apply My life to it. Wait for My presence, to move. Rest in Me. See My work being done in all situations. Be free by My Spirit, and you will have an abundance no matter what the outward circumstances might appear to be.

"How is it that nothing seems to change? The world gets darker, and I feel farther from You, more helpless — no matter what I do."

Holiness, denial of self, sacrifice, and the crucified life — why do you not seek them? They are the true path to happiness. You fight to protect those things you hold tight and call it My work. You walk without power because you have not made Me your source of power. You are ineffective by My standards, but your search to fulfill your personal needs blinds you from seeing how barren your life really is! In doing your work and calling it Mine, you have become angry, fearful, and "in need" of changing your world. How foolish! How vain.

I am seeking those who cherish holiness unto Me. I will use those who turn from this world and its ways. Despise those things which stop you from giving up your life completely to Me.

"But Lord, it seems that the things of the world have such a hold on me — not really bad things, but things that distract me from really seeking You. I feel so bound, so torn."

Holiness is freedom for you. When Jesus was with you on Earth, He never set His mind on the things of the earth. My purposes and My goals were always His goals. As He kept His heart on things above, He walked through all earthly circumstances untouched. Even on the Cross He was untouched. There was no earthly power that put Him there. Schemes and dreams of mere men were of no effect, for He was not moved by them.

That same freedom is yours if you trust in Me. You need not be touched by that which is around you. Surrender fully to Me. Seek My purposes rather than your own. Learn of Me and My ways. Submit to My Spirit, that you might be free. The work that I plan for you is for your best interest.

Submit to it. You too can be untouchable if you keep your eyes on Me.

"But if I fully concentrate on You, I look like a fool. I can't just stop what I'm doing. How will I live? Surely You don't expect me to give up everything?"

When did I ever say that ease and comfort would be your lot? Look into My Word. Those that I called My own, those I held dear to My heart, at times had no place to live. Even My own Son had no comforts of this world. You seek to satisfy your own needs and call it My will for you. I prosper you, and you use it to pad your rest areas.

Do you not see that I cannot use you with a heart that has grown cold? The weight of your possessions and lusts and fears of loss have nullified your testimony. You look no different than the world.

Change your hearts now. Turn from seeking Me for your own gain. The selfless life is the life I have called you to. You gave Me everything; why do you take it back?

I want to use you for My purposes, but you are too busy serving your own needs. The people perish all around you, and you don't even look up from your toil. You praise Me with your lips, but your hearts are far, far from Me. Return now that I might use you.

"But I thought I was doing Your work. I thought You told me to show the world its sin. I am trying to be an example for You, to bring people to You."

From My perspective, some of you are acting no differently than the world that is perishing. You are using its methods to change its unchangeable heart. Why would you think that true, lasting change can be accomplished by the ways of man? Laws never change hearts, for the heart is wicked. When you move in the flesh, fleshly changes result.

I have never called you to pursue anything but Me. When you do that, we move in the spiritual realm to change hearts to save those who are perishing. My Word shows how fallen man is helpless to even see the need to repent and change his ways. My Word shows how My covenant is invoked when My Spirit moves on the heart to come to repentance. When that happens, eternal changes result. That is My way. You cannot see, however, because you want changes your way; and you are ineffective, because I cannot be with you to empower you because it is not My way. It never will be.

I have one purpose for you now that you are Mine. It is the purpose My Holy Spirit, who is now in you, has always had. He has always proclaimed the beauty of Jesus to a world out of answers, a world dying in its sin. He has always moved so that those who are perishing might see, and come and be saved. Why are you not moving in that same direction? All else that seems important is folly. I am not in it. Why would you be?

"But I thought I was moving with You. I'm involved. I thought that was Your work."

Where is the weeping at the altar? Where is the true denial of self? Where is the desire for a crucified life? How long do you think I should tarry? How long do you feel I should hold back My judgment?

I have called you and entrusted you with My Word, My light to your dying generation, and you have only served yourself. Soon your fleshly desires will be shown for the little value they really are. Buy from Me gold refined in the fire.

Turn from your ways. They are far from My ways. Turn now. The time is short!

"If that is true, Lord, what do we do? Where do we go?"

Your nation has turned its back on Me, and you attempt to change it in your own strength. How foolish. Don't you see that I have given it over to its own sin that it might be consumed? I am not in its folly. Why should you be?

You, My people, have held abominable gods close to your

55

heart. You have befriended the idols of the land. As I deal with your nation, you will be purged, you will be purified. There is still time for you to find safe harbor in Me. Rend your hearts; weep for your sin. Turn from your idols. Stop useless activities to protect yourself. There is no protection other than Me.

Seek Me, for I am safety. Seek Me, for I am power. Seek Me, for I am the only stronghold for your children. Stop and think. If I lifted My hand, what could you do in your strength to change that? Open your eyes and see.

"Oh Lord, show me what I need to do. Open my eyes that I might see. Create in me a clean heart, and renew in me a right spirit. Show me. Change me as You promised. I feel helpless; I don't know how to change. I don't know where to start or what to do. Help me."

Your carnal mind cannot begin to understand what I have planned for you. I call you My children. That you can understand. When My glory is manifested, My Word says you will be as I am. [see I John 3:2]

If you could only believe. If you would only come close enough that I might express Myself to you. Your eyes are big towards what is happening around you. In your disloyalty, the world is powerful. In your obedience, you can see a little more of My perspective. There is nothing too hard for Me. There is nothing to fear if you choose intimacy with Me over activity in the flesh. My plans for you — who you are now and what you shall become — do not depend on the world and its ways. They are not changed by loud voices.

Understand: I do not change. I do not waiver. I do not fail. My Word is true and at work even now in the din of life. To see My purposes, you must turn to Me. I don't mean for you to pray about things;* I ask you to come to be changed.

I am not interested in what you do, as much as I am interested in who you are becoming. How can old things pass away if you remain in them? You are no longer part of this world. Separate yourself from it, for it is soon passing away. Only My Word, My ways will remain. Come to Me now. I love you.

"Yes, Lord."

*Editor's note: when turning to God.

Who Will be Empowered?[13]

My children that thrive on and desire only intimacy with Me are about to be empowered with My presence. Those that have turned away from their useless flurry of activity to change the world are about to enter into a spiritual understanding that will allow them to again represent My Son Jesus to their world. People will recognize My Son through their lives. They will see Him and have to choose between life or death because of the convicting power of a wholly surrendered vessel of honor that contains My Holy Spirit. Who can deny what has been done for all mankind when it becomes visible through the lowly, the weak, the surrendered, the children.

I will not use the dead, the empty, and the proud. I never have and will not start now. Whitewashed containers full of dead men's bones have no place in the economy of spiritual power. I have called you. Now I am about to empower those who have come.

4. Getting Ready

A. How Can I be Led by God? —

How Can I be in God's Perfect Will?

Insensitive

Oh, how My heart is grieved. Oh, how hurt My heart is as time after time you are insensitive to Me and My words and My directions, wooings, and callings. You rush on and over things, with your mind set on other things and desires. Your will is set on what your heart desires and plans. You are insensitive to what I am saying to you at the moment. Many times you actually run over My plans and My will for you. Your wills are strong. Your minds are set on what you think you need and want.

Oh, if you'd only wait and listen. Quiet yourself. Slow down. Stop; listen. I will lead you in the right direction and the right way. Do not lean to your own understanding. Do not trust in your own way. I will develop My sensitivity in you as you come and cry out for My character to be formed in you, and as you desire My will above your will.

Wills of Iron

My children, My children, I do not know if you realize the supreme importance, the supreme importance of your yielding to My direction and My will for your life. I am coming to you and asking as your Father, asking as your beloved Bridegroom, asking as your Teacher, that you would yield yourselves and your will to Me. It is of utmost importance at this time. There is a steelness, a stubbornness in your will; it is strong. It is like iron and steel. You have set your ways and your hearts and your thoughts and your emotions on one thing and on one purpose, and it is hard for you to see that I am directing you and I am pulling you another way.

Oh My children, My beloved children, do you not see and do you not sense that the harness I am placing upon you is for your good and not for evil? Do you not see that I know what is best, I know what is ahead, I know the plan that I have for you? I know your part in these Last-Day workings. Your mind is so set on what you think and what you have reasoned out and what you have done in the past; and because of these feelings in your flesh, you have allowed yourself to think it is My will. You are set in your ways. You are set in your ways, and it will take an atomic bomb in the spirit, as it were, to blast you out of your way of thinking and your plan!

Oh My children, My children, do you not see and do you not hear and do you not sense that as you come to Me, as you come to Me for love and love alone, as you come and are willing to lay yourself — not anybody else, but yourself — before Me and prostrate yourself before Me, then you will know My direction and My leading? Are you willing to accept it if it is different than what you are thinking today? Are you willing? Will you be willing to accept it if it is not what you have thought and reasoned out and planned and are planning at this very moment? Are you willing? Are you willing to lay it all down at My feet and say, "Lord, I surrender. I surrender it all"?

My children, My children, I call you. I call you to My heart with love. I want for you to know My best and My utmost for you. And you will know, as you yield and as you come as a little child in total surrender and obedience to Me. You will know and you will see, for it will all come to pass as I have planned it to be.

A Call to Zealous Repentance

Mean business when I call you to do something for Me. It will require repentance, for your lives are filled with your own desires and comforts and healings. You try to heal yourselves; and in doing so, you pull your comforts close to your bosom and hang on tightly. Your comforts have many shapes and consistencies: They range from people, to animals, to possessions, ambitions, and even callings. YOUR thoughts, plans, and will — always you are focused on yourselves. You leave no room for even My suggestions. You have already determined what you can and cannot do according to what has always been in the natural concerning you. You leave no room for the supernatural working of My power. You leave no room for My voice and leading to "disrupt" your normal everyday happenings. You are crippled in spirit and choose to continue on in your own way — supported and coddled and comforted by your friends and your own decisions on what, how, and where you will do your and My business.

Wake up! You are selfish and self-centered! Your world revolves around you. What about My Kingdom and My Kingdom plans? What about them? I am calling you to zealous repentance. You will do no great work for Me until you are willing to submit to My chastening and correction. Your hearts are pining away to do a "work" for Me. You are struggling and maneuvering and selecting and planning.

Stop it! Get on your faces and repent. You aren't listening and haven't seen what I've been doing all these years in preparation to bring you to this place of service. You are still in the place of control in your life, unyielding and unwilling to let go of your securities and your way of thinking and planning.

I call you to repentance and a laying down of yourself. This is not a call to rush out to do a service for Me and gratify yourself. This is a call to lay yourself down and to let go of everything of you, and let Me do the chastening, refining, purifying work I desire to do in you. I can only do it as you abandon yourself to Me and obediently submit to all that I ask of you — in every area.

Don't you see? You are too valuable to Me to not do this work. Let Me, the Potter, make you again into another vessel — molded and shaped according to My plan. Let go. Let go. Do not hold on to even a tiny shred of what you figure is okay. Give it all to Me — all areas — and let Me do a work which you could not believe even if it were told you. I desire you for Myself. I alone shall prepare you for service, but I must know you are entirely Mine — yielded, obedient, submissive.

So Few Marys

Marthas — good, well intending Marthas — but so few Marys. Many have so much to say, but few can listen. Few can quiet their busy selves long enough for them to develop a deep and intimate friendship with Me. Few care to sit to hear My words — just to be with Me. Most want answers or directions, but few want to spend time like Mary did, just to be with Me and listen to Me. I have so many things to tell you of Myself, My Word, and the Father.

Get to know Me. Get to know the Comforter, the Holy Spirit. He will tell you all things, for He does not speak of Himself. He will relay the messages. Your directions and answers will flow freely and naturally from these times. You will not need to be anxious or concerned. You will know what to do, where to go, what to say — ahead of time, many times. It will come as you have these sacred, cherished, quiet times. Guard them. They are your place of refuge. They are chambers of love.

Check with Me

Just because you think something is right for you (because it is exactly what you like according to your taste) does not mean that in the long run it is best for you or will be the most useful for you. Trust in Me. I know what is best for you in the long run and what will prove to be most useful for you. Besides, I know your future; I have the Master Plan. Check with Me, for I will lead you and guide you into all truth.

Check with Me in the morning about your day. I will cause you to know those things that I want you to be aware of. Listen very carefully. If you feel alerted about anything, know that I have warned you. Keep a close watch on things. Keep checking with Me. The enemy of your soul would seek to ensnare and entrap you and hinder My plan. I will alert you, but you must be aware that I am speaking. Do not overlook My leadings. Act on that which I show you.

I want you to share and confide in Me in every little thing you do or say, or plan to do, each day. I care. I'm interested. Don't hold back or think I'm not interested. Not holding back — sharing every thought and longing and desire — is a big part of love. What you are doing and plan to do today — the fact that you will check with Me and include Me in it — is exciting to Me. It's telling Me that you want Me to know where you are and what you are doing, in case I call. It's telling Me that I am an important part of your day and all the happenings in it. It is the way I become a part of you all day long.

Be Still and Listen

Be still, be still and listen to what I have to say to you. It is so important for you to listen. Your guidance will come through listening. Your peace will come through listening. Be still, wait, and listen. Don't rush on or ahead in excitement or eagerness. Draw aside to be with Me, and come and quiet yourself before Me and listen. Just the fact that you choose to draw aside and sit with Me brings such joy and pleasure to My heart. And just the fact that you care enough to come and sit with Me — just to be with Me — delights My heart. It is an expression of your love for Me. Lovers love to listen! There is an eagerness to hear what their beloved has to share. True lovers will listen with their heart.

I need you to be still and listen. I have much to share with you. There is much on My heart that I need to share, and will only share with those who are willing to pull away from the busyness of the things they do in My Name. Oh the wasted effort and mistakes that are made because they will not draw aside and quiet themselves in My presence.

You Are Not Really Listening

You are not listening. You are not really listening. You are only hearing what you want to hear. You are not acting on the thought I bring to your mind. You run right over it. You don't even stop to consider it. I want you to learn that the impressions and thoughts that I bring to you are for a reason. I am alerting you. I am trying to let you know things in advance, but you go on the same way. When I speak, I want you to speak. You are hesitant and holding back.

Insensitive — you are insensitive to Me. You do not know the value and the far-reaching effect of what I am saying to you and impressing you with. If only you would speak the thought I put in your mind. Your self-consciousness keeps you from expressing your thoughts and feelings many times. You are so worried and focused on what you are saying and trying to think of saying, that you are missing My direction.

Self, self, self! You put little value on what I say. It's almost as if it doesn't matter or isn't really that important. I love you. I need you to feel the full impact of what I am saying to you. Only as you correct this by recognizing it and repenting of it and setting your heart to be careful and cautious, will you overcome it. It is part of dying to yourself and your fears and stubbornness. As you die to yourself and your own thoughts and will, this insensitivity will die.

Respond

You are not responding quickly enough to My promptings in your inner man. You question, and doubt comes in, and you become double-minded; and it's downhill from there. You get worn out, and confusion comes in; and you wander off the path. "Is this the way; is that?"

I can save you a lot of steps and confusion if you'll listen for My direction in your inner man. Cast out doubt and confusion and fear, and listen for My gentle leadings. Sometimes I only nod My head in the direction I want you to go. I know the timing involved. The answer has been held up. Press in for it!

Obey

You are reasoning things out in your mind. You are not acting upon the impression I give you [when in prayer or after you've been in prayer concerning something].* Then doubt and fear come in. You listen and consider and contemplate the lies of the enemy concerning a situation, and then confusion comes in and, with it, a struggle. You entertain vain imaginations and vain notions, which you set above My thoughts and plans for you.

I have given you instructions on how to make decisions. I said My people shall not be confounded. If you do not act immediately on what I show and tell you, you step into wavering, which is dangerous and will thwart My plan or destroy it.

You are guilty of reasoning things out. When I speak, obey. Do not grieve My Spirit. Proverbs 3:5 says, "Lean not unto your own understanding." You will not understand everything. Trust Me that I know what I am doing, and I will work all things together for your good.

*This truth applies *only* to someone who has a FULLY developed prayer life, which would include a daily secret closet of prayer.

[The person who received the prophecy speaking]: "We are only seeing surface things in many circumstances. Things can be very different than what we perceive with our natural minds. That is why it is so important to trust God's leading, direction, and word. It is imperative that we obey, because so many things are deceiving and deceitful. Only God knows the true purpose and thoughts in any given situation. If we go by what we see or feel or conclude according to the natural mind, we will be deceived."

[God speaking]: You can trust your Father. Stop struggling. Listen, obey, and follow. I am working out My good plan and purpose and My good pleasure.

I Have You in a School

My children, I have you in a school: a school of training, a school of discipline, a school of love. Thus far you have done those things that have been required of you, those things that have not seemed out of the ordinary, or that, in many cases, have not even seemed necessary. They have been things that have been required. And you have seen them as such: things required of you. But I am training you, and I am wanting to train you for a very specific schooling, a very high calling, a very high grade of schooling; and I am training and shaping and molding you for that, even at this time. It may seem intense to you. It may seem beyond your reach at times. But I am calling you, preparing you for specific tasks, specific hours, specific needs.

And I will give you specific instructions. I am training you to hear My voice at all times, training you to hear My voice second by second, step by step. You are walking out into a world full of land mines — hidden mines in fields, in your paths. If you do not hear My directions clearly, if you do not listen for each one in a very specific way, you will have things literally blow up in your face — as you go that way, as you rush on, as you hurry on, as you carelessly go on.

So I'm training you to be careful, My children, because the days that lie ahead will be days of much darkness, great darkness, gross darkness! There will be so much confusion around you, so much noise, so much clamor, so many things calling out to you in the natural — things that seem right, things that seem good — that you will fall, you will fail, and you will be entrapped and ensnared many times, if you are not hidden with Me; that is, if you are not used to and accustomed to going to that place of quietness — that place where you are hidden with Me, and Me alone, for love, and love alone, to know Me and to become deeply acquainted with Me, to become united and to be in union with Me.

So this intense training is to get you ready. And do not fear it. Do not fear it. It is glorious, My children. Just think: you — you led by Me, by My Spirit. You will not move unless or until you know it is your time to move. So many times, already, I've spoken and you have questioned it. You've questioned it. It has held you back, and it has led you into places where you didn't even want to be, and you were miserable there. But know, My children, that it will not be your natural human reasoning leading you. It will be this gentle love, this gentle voice of love, the voice that you are getting to know as you sit at My feet, as you gaze into My eyes.

Do not be afraid of these days ahead, My children, for you will not walk in fear; you will walk in love, led by My Spirit — led around, led through, led over, hidden. You will actually be hidden at times. People will not even see you in times of danger, even though you are there!

Can you believe this, My children? Can you believe this? But you must prepare, you must respond today — step by step. My Word is a lamp unto your feet and a light unto your path. The steps will take you onto the path and will keep you. But know, My children, that up to this point, in many, many instances you've done only that which is required of you, only that which has been required in the daily ordinary doings of your life. But I have much more. I have much more — secret things. And you are being trained in this Army, as it were, and it will be a very high calling, a *very* high calling.

So come away, come away, My beloved, to that place where you are trained and where you will know that I am your only love, because you have been willing to lay down everything else — and that's the only reason why you will come

—in every area, in every arena of your life.

At times you're going to feel like you are in a ring with boxing gloves on, fighting off these other things. But know that it's possible — possible by My Spirit and because you love Me. You will fight off every other love with boxing gloves, as it were, because you won't want anything else to get a hold on you, nor anything else to be in any kind of running, neck-in-neck, with My love for you. And as you do that, I will give you what you need to be sustained, and it will be right, My children; it will be right. It will not be tarnished or tainted by anything of this world. It will be right.

So let Me lead you. Do not lean to your own understanding. Trust Me in every circumstance, and desire to hear My voice, and you shall hear Me gently calling you, teaching you, instructing you, and leading you.

I Will Instruct You

Did not I instruct Noah how to prepare before the great flood? Did not I give him specific and detailed instructions on how to prepare the ark? Did not I wait patiently while he carefully followed and carried out My instructions?

I will instruct thee and teach thee in the way which thou shalt go. I will guide thee with Mine eye. But you must be careful to closely follow My instructions. Listen carefully and prayerfully for My voice, for My instruction, for My warning. My Word is a lamp unto your feet and a light unto your path. Remember, it is a lamp and a light. When things get very dark, My lamp and My light will lead you. My voice will direct you. My Word will order your steps.

A time of great darkness is coming upon this earth — as foretold by the prophets and sages. It will be very dark! Darkness will prevail. My light will be the only light. The world is secure now, and there are many lights, brilliant dazzling lights, alluring and sensual. Multitudes run to them, only to be swallowed up in them and overcome by them. But they are temporal and will soon pass away. And there will be great darkness. Many will perish in that time of darkness!

In the days ahead you will have many decisions to make. Many choices shall be presented to you. It is only as you stay close to Me and continue in My Word on a daily basis that you will be able to make the correct decisions and the right choices. Cling fast; hold tightly to Me. Love Me with all of your heart.

4. Getting Ready

B. Spiritual Warfare:
The Battleground of the Mind — How to Win It

Targeted by the Enemy

I tell you, My children, and I warn you that you have been targeted by the enemy because you are seeking Me with all of your heart and you are desiring to draw close to Me and to cleanse your heart. Those who are walking this path of submission and surrender and repentance will be especially targeted by the enemy. And at all times they are in counsel, they are in meetings, they are continually gathered together for war against you, to shoot out their arrows at you. So I want you to be aware and alert to this fact.

But although you are targeted, and although you may be marked as a person that the enemy is wanting to hit, it does not mean that you are not covered. Because, as you continually come to Me and seek My face and My guidance, and as you desire and ask Me to lead you in the way that you should go — to teach you the path that you should take, to lead you in the truth and to teach you — and as you wait on Me continually and check with Me; know that I will alert you and I will make you aware of these things. And as you draw close, and as you are willing and wanting your heart to be cleansed, more and more, when you are attacked, when these fiery darts hit you, you will find that you hate these things that come out of you. You will hate the strongholds that the enemy has built up and your reaction to his arrows, instead of responding according to My Word.

Know this, My children, that the work I am doing in you now and the call that I am calling you to, is the call of repentance, it is the call of cleansing, it is the call of purifying. And only as you cleanse and purify your heart, can I reveal Myself more clearly to you. Only then can I use you in the way that I desire to use you. For there are still things in your lives that I am working on and working at. But I can only do this as you respond and yield yourself to Me. Yield yourself to Me. I will be your shield, I will be your fortress, I will be your armor, as you are diligent in seeking Me and My face.

So, as I have told you before, do not be afraid and do not be discouraged or dismayed, but be alert; be alert and know that what you are doing and how you are seeking Me is making the enemy angry. You are a prime target for him because of the work that is being done in your heart. It is two-fold: the work being done and the work I have ordained for you to do. But you will not and you cannot do this work unless your heart is thoroughly prepared and unless your heart is all Mine and your lips are clean and your hands are clean and your heart is pure.

So do not be discouraged but press in even more diligently to Me and to My Word, in that secret place of prayer, where I can speak to you and show you the areas that need to be searched, that need to be known, and that need to be tried; so that we can eradicate, as it were, these things from your life — so that you can be used as a clean and powerful vessel that is dead to self and alive to Me.

Distractions

Do not be discouraged, My children. Keep looking unto Me. Lift up your eyes and open your ears unto Me, the Spirit of the Lord your God, who is wooing, speaking, and drawing you. Just as you are experiencing distractions and noise and even harassment, so it is in the unseen realm of the spirit all around you. Daily, hourly, every minute, the enemy is seeking to destroy. He is seeking to come in to get your mind off of Me and off of hearing My voice and My direction for you. He is bringing in many things, and even though it may seem calm and peaceful around you, in the spirit world there is much going on, much to distract you.

There are meetings, there are planning sessions on how to distract you and how to get you off the path that I have planned for you, how to thwart you from My purpose and My plan and My will, how to get you to listen to other voices. And although up to this time they have not been distracting voices that you could actually put your finger on and say this is distracting me in a special way, and although there has not been harassment that you have felt and there have not been people pounding on your door, as it were; yet, you will experience it, My children. The time is coming when these forces will become so strong in and around you that you will actually feel like you are in a room with a closed door and people are pounding on your door wanting to get in, pounding on your door wanting to carry you away, pounding on your door wanting to trip you up or find a word that you might say that would make you sound like you are guilty of something.

These things are coming, My children, and this is just a small foretaste of what's ahead. So I am causing you to be alert to the things that are coming.

You must diligently prepare your heart. You must know Me above all other voices. You must know Me above everything, because if you don't, your very heart will be deceived because some of the voices will be so deceptive. They will come in a way that is smooth and flattering, and you will be deceived because behind them you will not hear the loudness of that knocking or that voice. It will be covered over. It will be deceptive. It will be in the form of a masquerade, and you will not know.

You will be deceived and carried away with this flood if you are not now clinging to Me, if you are not now desiring Me with all of your heart, if you are not now seeking to know Me above all things, if you are not now willing to lay down everything. Everything! Every desire, every need, every love. If you are not desiring at this time to lay that down and to turn from these things and to abandon yourself to Me and to die to yourself, you can very easily be deceived.

My children, listen. Listen to the voice of the Spirit. Listen for My Spirit as He speaks to you this day, as He comes in His gentleness, as He comes in mercy, as He comes in love, wooing and calling you to separate yourself and come to Me with all of your heart. For the days are coming, and will be here very soon, when you shall have no other place to go. Hide yourself in Me now. Hide yourself in Me: your Rock, your Ark, and the Lover of your soul. Hide yourself in Me.

A Spirit of Deception

I am coming so very, very soon. Yea, watch and see, My people, watch and see. Yea, you shall see great, great, great signs; you shall see signs and wonders, yea, and they will not be of Me, saith the Lord God. Be very cautious as to where you build. Be careful and pray about everything, for there are many deceivers in the world and there are many deceivers in My very own Church, saith the Lord God. Be cautious of people, saith the Lord. Yea, watch, watch their signs; compare them with Me, for My Spirit indwells you. My Spirit will lead you and guide you and tell you what is truth and what is error, saith the Lord God.

Yea, for you shall be anointed by Me from On High, saith the Lord God, and I shall give you strong discernment;* and you shall hear words that people speak, and those words will

73

not be My words. But you will compare them to My Word, and you will know that they are not My sayings, that they are made up by these people, saith the Lord God. For a spirit of deception has crept in upon My people, and many are being deceived! Yea, for My people think that they should follow these words that they hear, and My people will be wrong! But I am giving you this strong discernment that you will be not be led astray, saith the Lord God.

Yea, so watch and see, and listen to the words that are spoken in prophecy, for not all prophecy is of Me, saith the Lord God, for some comes even from the flesh. So be very, very careful and listen to every word that is spoken and compare it with My Word. And I say this unto you: that many, many, many shall hear My voice, but many, many (listening to other voices) shall fall away! saith the Lord God.

But I am drawing you to a closeness to Me, saith the Lord God. So stay very close, stay close to Me, for I have much work for you to do. And My power shall come upon you; My power shall fall upon you to do the works that I want you to do. So stay close to Me and seek My face daily. Pray daily, saith the Lord God, and keep your hearts clean, for I have much work for you to do in a short period of time, so very, very soon.

So look for Me, saith the Lord God, and do not look for the terrible times, but look for Me. For I am the Deliverer, and I will set people free. So stay close to Me, and keep yourself humble and pure before My very eyes, saith the Lord God.

*From drawing close to the Lord and staying close to Him.

Note: For more on this subject, see the prophecy, "A Solemn Prophetic Warning," in the book, *Prophecies of the End-Times*, pages 178-186.

Do Not Become Entangled

My children, do not become entangled in the things of this life. For I have set before you a path, a path that you will walk. It is the path of life, and you must run on this path, run with patience on this path of life, but the enemy would seek to entangle you along the way. There are many entanglements that he would seek to catch you in, many things that you will sense and feel. For even now you feel as if you are cutting your way through brush with your hands out before you, just trying to make your way through a thicket or a maze or something that is hard to get through as you are running.

But I would say to you, My children, do not become entangled. Keep your eye upon the goal, for there is a path that is set before you, a race to run, and a prize to obtain. But it will be a struggle at times, as you keep your eye upon the goal, because there will be many voices calling to you along the way as you run on this path — many voices and things that will call to you, and they will affect your feet, they will affect your body and your mind. They will be as entanglements that will entrap you and ensnare you, and they will draw you off. They will seek to draw you off from this path, the path that I have called you to run on, the path that I have called you to walk on, the path that grows brighter and brighter, that leads to Me and to eternal life.

Do not be enticed, do not be drawn off by the lusts of your very own flesh. Do not be drawn off. Examine them and know that as I call, I enable you to run. There will be a beating off, there will be, in many instances, a breaking through these things that would seek to entangle you. And I speak this to you this day as a form of caution and warning, that you would be aware that there are things that will seek to entangle you. But you are as the runner, you are as the runner that is determined in his mind to run this race. You are running it even now, and these things will come before you and call to you in all areas, all areas. They will seek to entangle you.

So, only as you continue to seek My face, only as you listen to My Word and know that My Word is the Word of Life on this path of life that will keep you, only then will My Word keep you, My children, from falling into these different entanglements and snares. My Word will keep you from veering off course and from being drawn off the course that I have set before you. It is not something to fear. It is not something to think you cannot do, because I am your Father and I am calling you, I am instructing you, I am wooing you, and I am giving you the things that you need to keep you strong. As you continually come to Me to love Me, to worship Me, to adore Me, to hunger and thirst after Me, you will be kept on that road.

But it is the lust of the flesh and the lust of the eyes and the pride of life that will entice you and draw you away, draw you off that path that I would have you on. Be careful, My children. Continue to come to Me, continue to lift up your eyes, continue to desire to hear My voice and to walk in My ways and to be instructed. Continue, continue to want Me and My Word more than anything, and I shall speak to you and keep you on the path that you need to be on. You need not fear it.

To Overcome Sin[14]

The lusts of the flesh and the pride of life allow the enemy to gain access to you. They make you vulnerable to attack by opening the door to any form of fear and oppression. You *must* overcome them.

There is hidden sin in your heart. Remove it by repenting [of it] to Me. Let the light of My Holy Spirit shine on it. Confess it as sin, and turn from all entertainment of thoughts, sights, or habits. Renew your mind daily with My Word, My thoughts, and My presence; and you will be set free. You turn away [from sin], and I will be there for you, but you must turn away. Each time a thought is noticeable cast it down. Stop looking in the direction of sin. Stop holding it dear, for it has no place in you. You are Mine, and I want you spotless. I am jealous for that area of your heart.

Come to Me and be holy. In My holy fire, any presence of evil will be consumed. I am your safety, your strong tower, your haven. I am your consuming fire! I require you this day, return to your first love: your consuming love for Me, the desire for My Word, and the power that is Mine.

You know Me. Now begin to believe again. Flee from fear; it no longer has a hold on you. I have cut its cord, so turn from it. You are Mine and nothing will take you from Me. Be intense for My presence and My presence alone.

Avoid Breaches[15]

Holy ground is important to Me. There is no way for the unclean to enter if I have girded [My guardians] around My places. However, My back must be turned and My guardians must create breaches when vice is invited into My holy places by My children. Violations of My Word and the spirit of My Word by relaxed attitudes and thoughtless conversation bring forth harm and breach the safety of My protection. Guard your words, guard your relationships, guard your hearts, so that I might maintain My presence in your midst.

Because you are My children, there is no place that you are not safe if I have called you there, for I am with you. No one can intrude upon a place I have established for you if My presence is hallowed and welcome. But be assured that I am calling you to be watchmen over your words and your actions, that I might join you in all that you do, wherever you are, for your good and My glory.

Be Still

Be still, be still and listen. Do not allow yourself to be controlled by the hurtful thoughts Satan brings to you. As you accept and entertain them, they determine where your thoughts and emotions will be led. Do not fall into his trap; it is a pit and a snare. Once you've chosen to entertain his thoughts and listen to his voice, you no longer hear Mine the way you should. I keep speaking, but you have already been overcome by his hurtful, jealous, bitter, and merciless thoughts. And his thoughts are his will.

But I have a plan and a purpose and a calling for you. Do not struggle against it. Allow Me to break and crush your will so that My will for you can blossom forth. Do not be afraid to trust Me. Forgive and forget and go forward.

Testing Our Thoughts

I am leading you by My Spirit. When a thought or imagination comes, ask Me: "Is this thought of You?" Ask Me: "What is truth in this imagination?" Get the truth of the thought. Take that warning or direction and follow it. Act on it, be alerted, be aware of it. As a watchman you will be warned ahead of time by Me. You are learning. Continue in My Word. Continue in prayer. Continue seeking Me. Sensitivity to My voice and leadings comes from being in My Word and seeking My face.

Pushing Out Anxieties, Cares, and Concerns

I want you to know, My child, I want you to know this day and to be reminded in your heart that I have a great desire for you, great, great desire for you, and that I delight in you, My child, and that you are very precious to My heart, and that My eye is upon you, My eye is upon you day and night, and I watch over you with tender and loving care.

And I want to remind you that you are hidden in the cleft of the Rock, that I have placed you there and you need not fear. You need not fear that you will fall out of that place. You need not fear that you will be taken from it or dragged out, but know that as I have placed you there, I will keep you there. I will keep you in the cleft of the Rock, and I will strengthen you and sustain you there, and I will be with you.

I desire to reveal Myself to you in a greater way. I desire to reveal Myself to you in ways that you have not realized and have not experienced before. But as you continue to come to Me, My child, come to Me with your thoughts. Do not let these thoughts of the cares of this life crowd out My thoughts in your mind. Bring Me to mind; and bringing Me to mind will push out the anxieties and cares and concerns. For I want you to know that as I hide you and protect you, I will take care of that which your heart is concerned about.

Your heart is overcome with many things in many areas, and they seem greater than you can comprehend or figure out at this time. But know, My child, that I am at work, that I am working ahead of you; and that as you seek Me and desire Me more than anything, you will find that My plan for you and for those around you and for those you love, is a good plan; and know that all things will work together for good as you continue to seek Me. So just know, My child, that you are hidden, you are hidden in My love and in My care forever.

A Very Great Lesson

My children, there is a very great and important lesson that I want to bring home to your hearts today: It is the lesson of forgiveness. And it is so important that if you do not learn this lesson, you cannot proceed with Me. You cannot grow. You will not be in the place that I need you to be.

And the lesson is this, My children, it is this: that as you forgive, you are forgiven. But what you are overlooking today is that as you ask Me for forgiveness and I forgive you, then to those who ask you for forgiveness, you need to flow that same forgiveness. You need to acknowledge that forgiveness. I will use a very plain and probably homely illustration here today. As My daughter asked for your forgiveness today for things that she felt she had done wrong or maybe had offended you in, not one of you said, "You are forgiven." Not one of you acknowledged her asking for your forgiveness.

Don't you see the picture, My children? As I hung on the Cross, the thief asked Me for forgiveness, and I forgave him and I said, "This day will you be with Me in paradise." Do you see what happens as you forgive? You are joined with that person. You are able to become one. Then you are able to flow with that person. But if you refuse to forgive, if you do not acknowledge that forgiveness, then you leave that person with a question in their mind forever: "Am I forgiven or not?" If you do not forgive, then you are still judging that person. You are not on the cross. You are not flowing forgiveness.

The Cross is mercy. The Cross is a forgiving spirit. Mercy is a forgiving spirit. Mercy is accepting and forgiving that person so that you can then be joined to that person. Do you see why you still struggle with bitterness and anger and pride? Because, as long as those feelings are still there and you do not accept and freely flow forgiveness to that person and accept them the way they are (even though they have not grown to the place where maybe you think they should be at that point), you block. You block because I cannot forgive you unless you have freely forgiven and accepted, in mercy, that other person. Even as in a marriage, unforgiveness will block your prayers from being answered. It will block prayers; it hinders. It hinders. Do you see how it hinders?

Oh, My children, if you do not learn this lesson today, you do not understand the Cross and you do not understand what I have done for you on the Cross. Do you understand? Do you sense what I am saying to you this day? I've been waiting and waiting for you to get to this place of understanding. For then you shall go forth.

So, in My love and in My mercy I come with this lesson for you today, My children. Will you accept it? Will you understand it? And will you forgive as I in My mercy have forgiven you? Even concerning those who wronged Me, who put Me on the Cross, I said, "Father, forgive them, for they do not know what they do." That is the kind of humbleness, that is the kind of meekness, that is the kind of mercy that I want you to have and to exhibit in your life. It comes only as you forgive as you have been forgiven.

Guard Against Woundedness

The purpose of the School of the Holy Ghost is so that you can become bread. I want you to become bread. Lay aside all preconceived ideas and all fleshly wants and desires, which cloud your mind and distract you. Keep your mind stayed on Me and My Word. Fight off and resist these other thoughts. Keep on track with Me and be on guard, and you will be led and fed and taught. Any area of pining or woundedness is an open target for the enemy. He has a field-day with it. It gives him easy access to you and causes you to take your thoughts off of Me and My Word and My love for

81

you. You then pursue and nurse and coddle and entertain and fret over fears, anxieties, untruths, misgivings, and sur-misings. They cover a wide range of subjects and events.

Guard against woundedness. When an arrow comes, begin to pray for that person. Flow forgiveness. Flood them with My fulfilling mercies. Ask for My will to be done in their lives. Commit it to Me, and trust Me that I am working for your good — as you seek Me with all of your heart. The enemy will seek to turn you off course. Immediately bring your thoughts back to Me by praying as I instructed you. As you do, I can then continue to lead you on in My ways and paths and truth. Otherwise you are veering off course, and things will not be clear to you. My way is a way of truth and clarity.

Oh, how much you miss in a day because you succumb to your own thoughts and feelings. You are led down a path of woundedness, self-pity, and self-preservation. Turn, turn and come and follow Me. Deny yourself. Crucify yourself daily and follow Me. Flow forgiveness, and walk in the way of truth and life and light. You will be amazed. Things will open up to you, and you will be led and fed. You will be-come bread — in your closet and out in your world. You will feed many!

Apply My Blood![16]

The enemy is always planning to enter — to steal, kill, and destroy. He is always plotting. He shoots his arrows and fiery darts to burn and destroy. But if he can enter through the door or windows, he plunders and kills!

KEEP YOUR MIND COVERED WITH THE BLOOD! Apply it. It is your *only* safeguard against him. Apply My Blood to the areas of the enemy's strongholds. Let the Spirit reveal to you, in your life and in the lives of those you are praying for, where the enemy is robbing, killing, destroying, and paralyzing. Many he has tied up, as it were. They are helpless and are being destroyed!

Cleanse your houses with My Blood. My people perish for lack of knowledge! They know not the power or workings of My Blood.

Overcoming the Enemy[17]

Prepare yourself against enemy attack. Cover yourself, your house, your family, with My Blood. The enemy is always working, preparing, and planning. Be ever on the alert! Be prepared! You overcome him with My Blood and the word of your testimony. You defend yourself with:

1. The covering of My Blood.
2. Knowing and speaking: What I am
    and do and have done.
3. Defending yourself with My Word.
4. Soaking yourself in My Word:

> Think on It.
> Practice It.
> Arm yourself with It.
> Use It.

If you wait until you feel his hot breath and hear his cries, it will be too late! Casualties and even death will occur to you and yours. Be sure all are in the Ark of Safety. PRAY MUCH IN THE SPIRIT. How else will you know what to do? How else will you know the plan? I have the plan — the plan of attack. I know his maneuverings and his advancements, for I am all-knowing. I will show you things to come. Otherwise you will be surprised and overcome — time and time again!

It is not enough to only lock your doors against his attack. You must be strong in Me. His fire will burn your house down if you have not planned, prayed, and protected! The enemy has spies, as it were. They will come in and find out your whereabouts and your plans and the lay of the land. Confer only with Me. Keep secret those things you possess: the lay of your land.

Remember the Blood is a protection — a wall of fire around you! The enemy cannot enter it or touch you in it. Know it also, its power and workings. It is your greatest defense against him. I overcame him with it. Use it, My children, use it! Do not be overcome with his wiles and stratagems. It is so important! My people do not realize or know the importance of it. Study and acquaint yourself with it. Stand in it. It is alive! It speaks!

Get on your horse, My children, and ride. Ride into battle with My Plan. You shall overcome! But you must know My Plan and be prepared. Remember these orders:

1. The Blood
2. The Word
3. The Spirit*

Pray much! Be on the alert, ever prepared, and ye shall not be overcome.

*And 4. The Name (Jesus). See pages 166 and 206.

The Blessing Is in the Blood[18]

. . . . To be blessed by Me is to have the Blood covering on you. This is absolute, divine covering and protection from every kind of evil, seen and unseen. . . . For everything that is Blood-covered is protected. Satan cannot touch anything that is covered with the Blood. It is as safe as though it were in Heaven. Put your possessions, your loved ones, and yourself under the divine covering of My precious Blood. Remind

Satan that that is where they are. Let him know, together with his evil demonic spirits, again and again that you are under My Blood covering.

The same is true of works done for Me. Those precious souls I have given you are under My Blood covering. All your works, your ministry, your buildings, your family, your equipment, all the works of your hand are blessed because they are included under My Blood Covenant — therefore they are under My Blood covering. . . .*

This dispensation of grace has the Blood covering, because it is sealed with My Blood of the New Covenant. It will terminate with the Rapture. After that, only those who give their lives as martyrs can be saved out of the Great Tribulation. In these Last Days, My Blood will work more powerfully in a greater way than ever before.

*Editor's note: They are, if we faithfully and diligently follow the instructions given in the previous paragraph.

Follow My Instructions

You need to obey and do as I direct and instruct. I will always give you the plan of attack, but you must be willing to follow My instructions and do that which I command you to do. You must not lean to your own understanding nor reason things out. You must not turn to the right hand nor to the left. You must follow closely My instructions. Keep filling yourself with Me and My words. Be ever ready and alert to do My bidding. Draw nigh to Me. Learn to discern My voice in all matters. As you draw nigh to Me, I will draw nigh to you. You must draw nigh to hear Me clearly.

4. Getting Ready

C. Mary or Martha — Which One Are You?

Busyness

There is a busyness that pervades and prevails in and around you. Busyness leads you in your thoughts, actions, words, and deeds. As a result, you charge out ahead and enter into territory and boundaries you would not have entered, had you prayerfully and quietly and submissively listened, waited, and followed Me and My instructions, My warnings and directions. Take heed; slow down; quiet yourself. Be on the alert at all times. Remove the clutter and clamor. Seek Me and My ways, and walk in them.

Slow Down

I am calling you to slow down and set apart a time for Me and Me alone: a time of quietness, a time of sitting at My feet and learning, a time of cleansing, purging, and purifying. I want all filth, debris, and putrefaction removed. I want your idol of self knocked down and destroyed. I am asking for all — cleansing in every area! I want you to face yourself and see how untamed and unruly and self-willed your emotions and your affections are, how fickle your love is. It is a stench in My nostrils! There can be no sweet aroma of prayer until these things are cleansed and removed. Allow Me to do this work. Come, meet Me in the quiet place. Listen, learn, obey.

Listening Time

You are always rushing on to the next thing. You are anxious about many, many things. You take the cares of the day upon yourself, and you carry them. Oh, when will you give them to Me and let Me help you? Let ME carry them. They are not too heavy for Me. They are not too great. Take My yoke; learn of Me. My yoke is easy, My burden light. I will help you. Give them to Me.

Ask for My help and direction. Inquire of Me. Keep in constant communion; keep checking with Me. I know how to proceed, when to stop, what pitfalls to avoid. I know all. I will direct; I will lead. Only let Me, allow Me. Don't rush on; don't rush ahead. **Stop. Ask Me. Listen. Obey.** Your thoughts are way ahead of the events of the day, and you take the care and the burden of them and become encumbered as Martha was.

I will show you how to overcome these things. Keep checking and asking. Keep giving Me your anxious thoughts, plans, burdens, worries, and cares. Rid yourself of these things, and walk with Me in sweet communion and fellowship.

Quiet Yourself

How do you think your words, actions, thoughts, and deeds will become still if you don't pull yourself away from them and quiet yourself? It is only as you physically pull yourself away from those busy activities and quiet yourself before Me that you will see how unruly you are in those areas.

Your very lives have become a flurry of activities. Rapid motions are characteristic of all that you do and say. It is only as you quiet yourself in My presence that you will see it all clearly. Your constant rushing, day after day, is not My plan. It will profit you nothing. Did I not tell Mary and

Martha that one thing is needful? Mary chose it. It is a response of love. It is the base and core of our love relationship. It speaks of love, honor, and respect. It tells Me that you care deeply. It tells Me that My words, thoughts, and instructions and teachings are of the utmost value and importance to you.

Come, My children. Come and sit quietly before Me and listen; listen and hear My word. Without quiet times, you will be tied in knots. You will be going in a thousand different directions and accomplishing very little. When you worry and take on the care of things before actually doing them, you have already begun to destroy yourself. Anxious cares will eventually kill you. Your body becomes tight with tension, and all the joy of tasks and jobs well-done is never realized. Come to Me. Give Me all your burdens and cares. I will give you rest.

Saturate Yourself with Me

I want you to diligently search My Word and seek My face. There are treasures of truth that I want to reveal to you, but I cannot. You are so busy. I want you to take time, whenever you can, to search the Truth, and prepare and train and gird up your loins with the Truth. There is much I want to show you and tell you, but you are encumbered with much care.

Set aside your evenings to be quiet and to wait in My presence. Take your phone off the hook, and in the quietness and in the stillness I will speak to you:

I will show you things to come.
I will teach you how to pray.
I will lead you in the paths that you will go.

Put Me first. Put Me first, and all these other things will be added unto you. The time is short. I am preparing My vessels for greater service.

Believest thou that I am coming very soon? Then quit ye like men and be strong. Prepare, train, surround yourself with My truth. My Word is truth. Only as you saturate yourself with Me will you know My direction. Then will you hear distinctly and clearly My voice saying unto you: "This is the way; walk ye in it."

I have a great and specific work for you to do, but you are not ready. Prepare, prepare, prepare! You will need power in prayer. You must know Who I am and what I can do. Without Me you can do nothing. You must go out and go forward everyday and every night in the power and authority of My Name.

Stillness

In the stillness you will know that I am God. In the stillness you will hear My still small voice speaking to your heart. I will not shout above the activity of your day; I am not in it. You will not hear Me above the din and clamor of busyness. You must come aside with great desire and longing, and quiet yourself and listen, for I will speak to you as you desire Me to. I will answer your questions. I will bring peace and rest.

In your time of discouragement you think you need a wind, an earthquake, a fire answer. Quiet yourself. I am waiting for you to come to the end of yourself and your reasonings. Come. I will speak to you those things you need to know.

My Marys

To the Church it seems like the "Marthas" are the ones who are doing something significant for Me and My Kingdom. There is movement and activity and outgoing personalities. There is much talk and planning and preparing. They see needs, and purpose to see them met. Immediate action is taken so many times. There is much rushing, and a flurry of activity surrounds and accompanies all that they do. I am not in or even present in their much and endless talking and activity! They are like restless waves of the sea beating upon the shore. It is wearisome to Me. The constant pounding of the waves causes erosion. They will wear out in their own busyness, and the end-result will be death and not life.

Oh, that I could find "Marys" with a heart that will seek, crave, and desire Me and Me alone — quiet Marys, content to sit and listen to Me, apart from the busyness and demands of the so-called Church and its work. If only I could find Marys content with Me — just Me and only Me — Marys content to sit and listen and learn, Marys seeking Me with first love, and content and determined to forsake all else. They will be despised and misunderstood. Their quiet, seeking ways will be ridiculed and rejected many times. They will suffer rebuke openly and be reprimanded by the Church as it rushes on to do the "work of God."

My Marys will not be enticed or drawn away from their quiet, steady, loyal pursuit of Me. They are answering a call of love. Their heart is set. Their eyes are fixed intently on their Beloved, and they are content only to behold Him. My Marys are listening. They listen and hear My voice and Mine alone. And they are content to wait until I call them.

It is My Marys who will be an important part of the out-working of My Plan in these Last Days. It is My Marys who will hear My voice — the voice of their beloved Bridegroom calling them to Myself and the Marriage Supper of the Lamb.

My Marys are even now in preparation, for "the bride has prepared herself." For she shall be arrayed in a fine garment, clean and white. She is preparing her heart. She is dying to herself and the things of this world. She is willingly laying down her life in preparation. She is becoming humble, meek, and merciful; and in doing so, her love for Me is being purified. This process is taking place in My Marys as they pull away from the din and clamor of the world, and answer My call of love to come and sit and listen and learn.

It is My Marys that I come to. It is My Marys who will be ready. They will hear My final call. They will be **raptured** from this world — **raptured** to meet their First Love, **raptured** to be with Me forever! O My Marys, My precious Marys. I can hardly wait!

4. Getting Ready

D. Drawing Closer

I Am Teaching You About Love

I am teaching you about love — how to love and be loved, the hindrances to love and being loved. But you need to understand My love for you, My deep, enduring love for you and mankind — the love that made Me say, "Not My will, but Thine be done." Calvary Love, it's Calvary Love — love that is willing to lay down its life, love that is willing to give its all. Nothing held back!

Listen, watch, and wait. I am teaching you about My love for you: a love that will not let you go, a love that is ever seeking and searching you out, a love that is waiting and longing for you.

I Have Singled You Out

I have singled you out, My children. I've singled you out from among many. I have chosen you, and I have called you unto Myself. I have called you to come.

And do not think of yourself as part of a large mass at this time, for I have singly chosen you specifically for Myself because I have seen in you a desire to know Me. And I have been working and calling and wooing you, and I have brought you to a place very close to My heart.

And you dare not even look around you to see what others are doing at this time, because I have chosen you — singly chosen you — chosen you out; and I want you to know that you are chosen out from among many. Just as I chose out the disciples for a specific task, to be with Me first of all, so I have chosen you.

And even though the way that I lead you "on the stairs," the way that I lead you upward to My throne, is not always easy, and the steps are irregular and the way is rocky and stony at times; still, I see your heart's desire; I see you coming, I hear you coming. And to Me it is precious, because you are My beloved and I love you. You are very special to Me. And even though at times now I know you don't feel that way, know that you are answering a call.

Do not turn back; do not even look back at this time. Continue to come, continue to come; for there is a great purpose and a great need in My heart for you. And as you come, and as you desire Me more than anything that you have ever desired, you will begin to see the outworking of My purpose and My plan — not only in your life, but in the lives of others and in the lives of those whom your life will touch, as you are willing and obedient and answer that call to come to My heart, as I woo you unto Myself alone.

You Are Very Precious to Me

Know, My child, that you are very precious to Me and that I love you with an everlasting love. It is with cords of love that I have drawn you, cords of love. You have never been out of My sight, for I long for you, My child, and I love you. You are very precious to Me, and I desire you. I desire to have all of your heart. And even though you feel like you have been such a failure, yet I see you today as My precious one who has returned to Me, My precious one whom I have waited for and longed for and looked for and called to these many, many months.

And you have come, My child, you have come. You have answered My call, and that's all I am asking of you at this time. For I call you to Myself, I call you to My heart, and I will give you the strength to stand against all of the attacks of the enemy. I will give you the strength. You cannot do it in yourself; you cannot even think to do it in yourself, but it is My grace and My mercy and My love, My boundless love, that will enable you to do it. It is as you come daily, My child. It is you beginning to come — even this day as you have come — not even knowing how you can do it, but you have come!

And I want you to know that it's just that way that it's going to happen — as you daily come, as you start just where you are, to read My Word and to seek My face and to come and to lift up your heart and say, "God, I want to love You with all of my heart. I don't even know how, but I know that Your Word promises that You'll help me, and that if I come, You will." And that's exactly how it will happen, My child, for I am going to put iron in your soul, My child — iron! Your feet will be feet of iron, your shoes will be shoes of iron, and you shall stamp upon the enemy!

But it's as you come, My child. It's not some magical thing or even a formula. It's not some fantasy that you hope will happen some day, but it's that coming with all of your heart. Say, "God, I only want You. I only want to love You, I only want to serve You." And if I keep you enclosed, My child, for Myself for a season, do not despair. Do not think, "Oh, I want to do this or that for you, God." Do not despair. I want to bring you in to be a garden enclosed unto Myself. I want to minister to your heart and heal all your wounds, and I want to receive your love as you come to Me, because you come in weakness. I, I will make you strong.

Do you see, My child, I have reserved you for Myself. I

94

reserved you because I love you and I see in you that which I need. I need you. I need you to bring others to Me, that they may be reconciled just as you have been. But it will only come as you daily come — just for Me, just to love Me, just to want to know Me. Then it will all flow from you. It is not a heavy thing, but it's LOVE. It all has to do with My love for you and My Son's love for you, but I will help you. I will help you. Do not be afraid. Do not dismay, for you are going to stand tall and strong, and you will do a work for Me that I have reserved for you, and you alone, to do. But I will lead you out from that garden, that garden enclosed, where you and I will be together in deep fellowship and intimacy, for I love you, My child. I love you, and I will always love you; and I will never leave you, I will never forsake you.

You Are Very Desirable to Me

You are very desirable to Me, My child. You do not see yourself in that way. For many, many times you run, as it were, to make yourself look more desirable. You are running and checking to see if you are desirable enough to be accepted by Me. I want you to know, My child, that I desire you. You have never been more desirable to Me than you are right at this moment. And at this time you would throw up your hands, as it were, and say, "Me? Now? Look around Me. Look what's happening! How could I be desirable to you, Jesus?"

But I want you to know, My child, that you are desirable to Me, that I desire you. I have made and formed you the way you are, and I desire you. You do not have to fix yourself up, as it were. You do not have to be like someone else. You do not have to stand in their place. You do not have to say their speeches or do their things, because I desire you the way you are. You do not have to do anything to make yourself better, to make yourself be more accepted. You are accepted in the Beloved now, the way you are.

Run to Me, My child, run to Me. Run to Me the way you are, for My arms are open and I'm ready to receive you, I'm ready to hold you. I'm ready to embrace you in My arms just the way you are. You do not have to do something else to be received; your love for Me will be received just the way it is.

And as you do that, as you come without thought of how you might have to be or should be or might be, you will find that from that place of coming just the way you are (in your need, in your despair, in your despondency many times, in the clutter and clamor of the things around you); if you'll come just the way you are, to love Me — just because you love Me — you will find your way out of many of the things that you need to find your way out of. Because I, your Father, will lead you, I will direct you, I will carry you over some of these things. I will literally lift you up and carry you over some of them because of My joy, My joy and rejoicing over you. My heart rejoices over you, My child! My heart joys over you.

Do not hold back; do not hold back or draw back. Do not think that you are not worthy or you are not good enough or your position isn't right. Do not think that, for I have placed you and I have formed you and I am calling you. This call of love is to you, My child. Not tomorrow, not even tonight. This call of love is to you now! My heart is ever calling, ever calling, and it is a love call. The service will follow the love, so you must respond to this love call with all of your heart. Don't hold back — you're holding back your love. Don't hold back. Come, throw yourself into My arms! Just abandon yourself to Me and to My love, because I love you and I need your response. I am waiting for that total abandonment of yourself to Me and My love.

I Want You as My Bride

You never say "I love you" to Me. You take it for granted that I know. You assume you love Me, but you never really long to be with Me. You don't really desire My presence nor desire to be with Me. You really don't. It's all so business-like. It's not really flowing from your heart — heart-love — "mushy," over-powering, consuming heart-love. "Greater love hath no man than this: that a man lay down his life for his friends." [John 15:13] I did that for you. I loved you that much, and My love is still reaching out to you today.

Don't be afraid to love Me. Don't be afraid to be head-over-heels in love with Me. Think about Me constantly. Talk about Me to your friends; brag about Me. Talk to Me. Talk to Me affectionately, lovingly, often. Desire My nearness. Touch Me; embrace Me. I am real! My love is powerful, and My love is reaching out to you. I don't want to be your casual friend; I want to be your Lover! Friends are part of the wedding party but are never the bride. I want your intimate love — I want you as My bride.

This is Marriage Love

You are thinking of Me as being in Heaven, seated at the right hand of the Father, and you do not realize that I am with you. I *am* at the right hand of the Father, interceding for you, but I am also *with* you as your Friend and Lover, desiring you and wanting to carry on a torrid love relationship with you.

I told you in My Word that I would never leave you nor forsake you, and that I'd be with you until the end of the age. I do desire you. The desire you are feeling this day, "How can I express my love to you," is what I have been longing and waiting to hear from you. I do desire you. I do love you. I will not refuse you the kisses of My mouth — not a hen-peck kiss, but kisses of love and desire and affection. [see Song of Solomon 1:2]

Your response to My Name and the fragrance of it will grow more intense as you realize I love you. You! It's not an earthly love based on looks and education. I see your heart and your desire for Me. Don't be afraid. I won't reject you. I don't want you as My casual or even special friend; I want you as My beloved. This is marriage love: deep, intense, and single-eyed — My agape love issuing forth and pouring forth and desiring you. Come, come away, My beloved, to My chambers.

You Need Love Times[19]

You need *yada** times. How do you think intimacy with Me comes? You need love times: times of gentle whispers of love, times of gentle songs and praise. These times will bring you close to Me. I will embrace you. From these times will come My burdens, My secrets. From closeness and yearning for Me and My Word will come My burdens and My thoughts.

But you must have these *yada* times. How else will you really get to know Me? It will be in these times that your love for Me will grow and expand. It will bring a love and a union so close that at times we will not have to say anything. We will just embrace, and My love will flow to you, and your love will flow to Me.

I cannot emphasize enough how important these *yada* times are. They will bring you into a deep, deep intimacy with Me. I need to know that you are wholly Mine, that I can trust you.

*Yada: A Hebrew word meaning "to know." That is, to know intimately through close personal contact.

Leave Your Other Loves

What if My time isn't your time? What if, when I call you during the day, you don't hear or heed My call, and you go all day without taking times during the day to be with Me? Don't you long for Me — to steal away to be with Me during the day? Your prayers sound so sincere, but each day you fail the true test of love — stealing away to be with Me. You have a pattern, but it does not include shut-in love times of quietly being with Me.

I long for you to be with Me during the day — not only in the morning. I long for you in the evening and all night long. Your other loves call to you all day long and during the evening; and consequently they occupy your thoughts during the night hours also, because that is what you have given your heart to during the day — day after day.

Don't you really want to be with Me? Leave your other loves. Separate yourself from them. Divorce them, and love Me with all of your heart — all day long, all night long. I long for this intimacy. You hold back. You want Me, but only on your own terms. You have the heart of a harlot: You want Me, but you want your other loves also!

My Remnant Church

I am not an adulterer! I will not be married to a harlot Church! My eyes rove to and fro over the earth, looking for one who will stand in the gap; for through the prayers of one, I will take the poorest, dirtiest, bloodiest, almost-dead one and clean her up with My gifts of repentance and Salvation. As she turns to Me, seeking the face of her Master, I will create in her a clean, pure heart and give her holy hands to lift in surrender and worship to her Lord. I will take her with Me into the wilderness, and she will come out leaning on the arm of her Beloved.

My bride shall come from My Remnant Church. Today they meet in apartments and homes. Soon they will meet in cars, in caves, in shelters on the hills, in basements of burned-out houses, in shacks built from the rubble of destruction, in boats on the waterways, in dugouts on the desert's edge, in cleared jungle circles.

It is My Remnant Church that shall do greater works than I did. It is My Remnant Church that shall do mighty exploits. My new thing shall be done by My Remnant Church. To them alone shall I tell what is to come before I do it, and to them only will I reveal the deepest secrets of My Word.

Seek Me, My bride! Call out to Me! Long for Me; yearn to come into My heart! Desire Me to possess your heart to its very center! Oh, cry out for Me in the night hours, My bride. Learn of Me as Marys at My feet. Follow Me wherever I lead you. Surrender your will and all the desires of your heart unto Me. Be My faithful, true, and loyal bride. Have eyes only for your Jesus. I suffered and died and rose to life for love of you, My precious, pure, beautiful bride.

You Are Under a Nazarite Vow

Am I not speaking to you this day, My children, about separation, cleansing, purity, and holiness? Does not My Word say, "Be ye clean that bear the vessels of the Lord"? Have I not spoken that I desire truth in the inward parts, that in the hidden parts you may know wisdom? Do you not hear My call to sanctification, My children — to be set apart from the world and the things of the world, the call of the world, the food of the world, the drink of the world, the dress of the world, as I have spoken unto you?

I am calling you unto Myself to be chosen vessels to be used in this hour, to be used for a specific purpose and reason — according to My plan, purpose, calling, predestination, and will, which is already being done in Heaven and that I desire to be done here on Earth, in you and in this place. I am calling you to a place of separation and cleansing, My children. Allow Me, continue to allow Me to cleanse and purge your hearts.

Allow Me to shine the light of My Word on you. It's My Word that will bring conviction! It's My Word that will do the separating! It's My Word that will do the dividing! It's My Word that will do the piercing! Did I not say that now you are clean through the Word which I have spoken unto you? Allow My Word to do that work, My children, allow it. For My Word heals, My Word sheds light, My Word is a direction for you. It is what you need daily, minute by minute, on this pathway that you are treading.

Know, My children, that I am leading you on a narrow path. I am leading you on a narrow path for a specific reason: I am preparing you. I am using you now, but I am preparing you for an even greater work. But this is a testing time. You are under a Nazarite vow, as it were. I will ask you at certain times not to do things — to leave certain things off, to drop things, to exclude them from what you have done

101

before.

Do not listen to the voices of others, because they will not always understand what I am speaking to your hearts. But, as you seek Me earnestly, as you seek Me fervently, as you set your heart on the Lord your God to love, worship, and serve Him and Him alone, as you are faithful in resisting those things of the flesh that come up, as you are faithful in yielding to this cleansing and purging, and as you are asking Me to shine the light of My Word on your heart so that you can be cleansed; you will be transformed by My power, and you will be a fit and clean vessel, ready to be used in the way that I need you to be used in these last hours.

My children, do not cling to anything else. Do not look to the right or to the left. Do not look at your fellow brothers and sisters, even to see what they are doing. Walk according to the light that I shine on your pathway for *you*. For I have a specific plan for you, and I call you to do this.

And so, My children, do not be weary, and do not grow faint. You will grow faint as you look around you. You will grow faint as you look at the things that you want. You will grow faint as you look inside of you to your own desires. But as you look up and as you look unto Me, the Author and Finisher of your faith, and as you determine in your heart, above all, that you want to be acquainted with Me in all your ways, in all your doings, and all the way to the cross and the death of your self; then you will know Me and My purpose and plan, and you will be able to be used by Me in these last hours.

New Wineskins

The winevats are full — waiting to fill new wineskins, says the Lord. Do you not perceive the new thing I am doing, not only in your life and ministry, but in My Church? The work of sifting and shaking has been going on for years. Those who have had ears have heard and have allowed Me to turn their hearts in the direction that pleases Me. But many are still dull of hearing, content to remain in old wineskins.

But I say, My Spirit will be poured out and into new wineskins — vessels prepared through a time of testing and refining in the fire. I will have vessels that are pliable, not hard and brittle. There must be a softness and a willingness to bend to My will and My touch, says the Lord. Am I not the Master Potter? I will do the molding and shaping. I will do the crushing and the grinding and even the discarding. It is My decision how each vessel will be used.

Yes, the work of preparation continues. In some it is almost complete. The season is ripe for the wine from the vats to be poured into these ready vessels — into their new wineskins — so that they can then pour themselves out to others.

But, alas, many who are content to sit with old, brittle, worn-out wineskins will find that even if filled with the new wine, their seams would burst from the pressure. These are the very ones who would want to keep the wine all to themselves. So it is those who have softened themselves, who have humbled themselves under the mighty hand of God, that I will fill to overflowing in this new outpouring of My Spirit, says the Lord. Be ready, for the time is at hand. Be willing and be obedient.

The Remnant

"Let no man deceive you by any means: for that day shall not come, except there come a FALLING AWAY first, and that man of sin be revealed, the son of perdition." (II Thessalonians 2:3)

In these Last Days, deserters of the faith will fall away to the king of this world and go into eternal exile, away from God. But the Captain of the host of Heaven is calling and raising up a holy remnant — a holy remnant that is poor in spirit and that walks humbly with their God. This remnant is called to be vinedressers and soil tillers.

Vinedressers prune the vine and fertilize it to make it fruitful. This remnant will be used by God to call people to repentance and to holiness. They will be the mouthpieces of the Lord Jesus. This remnant will also be the soil tillers, who break up their own fallow heart ground, and call and teach others to do the same.

This remnant is poor in the eyes of the world, but rich toward God. They have absolutely no ties to the world and nothing to make the world envy them, but they have stored up true treasures in Heaven. Their hearts are Mine; their treasures and hearts are with Me alone.

This remnant will be mightily used by Me in these Last Days to show forth the exceeding greatness of My power to those who believe and to those who don't. ALL will know that I alone am God!

I Am Preparing My Remnant

I am preparing My remnant: I am cleansing, I am purging, I am purifying. I am drawing, I am wooing. This time of preparation is vitally important. The phases of preparation may seem hard and unreasonable at times. The strictness of My dealings and the severeness of My requirements may seem harsh and unbearable for the moment. But know that I am working out in you that which is necessary to bring you to a place of purity. The tasks I have for you to do can only be accomplished as you yield to the work that I am doing in you at this time.

I am bringing you to a place of humility, a place of lowliness, a place of total surrender and submission. You must be willing to submit to this breaking. It is a total emptying out of yourself. As this work is being accomplished, I will bring you face to face with yourself: your loves, your fears, your anxieties, your pride, your anger, your irritability, your bitterness.

You still struggle to be in control. You are not willing to die to it all. You will continue to struggle and strive until you are willing to die to it all. When you see your flesh rising up and leading and controlling, and you repent and cry out to Me to be broken and emptied out, when you are willing to trust Me with your very life, then I will be able to use you.

This is all part of the preparation. It is a walk of death to the flesh, so that the true, pure character of My Son Jesus may shine forth from you with a clarity and brightness that will witness and draw all men unto Me.

My Light in You

A time of great darkness is coming upon the land. It will be an evil and dark time. As the darkness increases, many will begin to look for light. They will not find it unless they come to the source of true light.

Did I not say that I am the Light that lighteth all the world? Light is sown in righteousness. My Kingdom is a kingdom of light. My Kingdom comes to you as you willingly lay down your life for Me. Your light will increase as you do the will of the Father on a daily basis. My light in you will increase as you are willing to yield and surrender all that concerns you and constitutes your fleshly will and desires. It is a life poured out, containing nothing of itself, wanting nothing for itself — a life abiding in Me, deriving its life, light, fellowship, and sustenance from Me, the Light of the world.

Men love darkness rather than light, because their deeds are evil. Let Me shine the light of My Word on your heart and expose all darkness, so that you may be, as children of light, a bright outshining of My love and life by which all men will be drawn unto Me, the Light of the world.

Allow Me to Break You

I made and formed you from the dust of the earth. I fashioned and designed you to use you as an instrument for My honor and glory. Even now I am shaping and molding; I am breaking and remaking. I am cutting and piercing, drying and staining. It is the work of the Master, Elohim — the creator and originator of all things.

Your vessel has become marred in the hands of the Potter. I am making it over again. The process seems long and hurtful and even hopeless, the pain intense and, at times, without comfort and balm. The circumstances surrounding you seem unjust and unfair. But all is from My hand. All I do is for your good. I must bring evil to the surface and work it out of you. I must separate the vile, before you will become pure and good — in thought, intent, motive, action, and response.

Your heart is still proud. You stubbornly hold on to your old ways and thoughts and purposes — but not willingly anymore. What you see and feel and speak are old hurts, wounds, anger, bitterness, lusts, longings, and imaginations. They have brought a hardness and arrogance and pride. Let Me, allow Me, to break you. Be willing to be shattered and brought low, so that nothing of your self is left — no hopes, no dreams, no longings, no loves, no defilements — just pure, tender, peaceable, merciful love. Then it will be all of Me and none of you.

The Path of Humility

My child, I am your Abba Father: your loving, kind, merciful, watchful, Heavenly Father. And I, as your Father, am leading you by a way that is different than what you thought or planned or could even imagine would be happening to you. But I, your Father, am in control, and I am in charge of your life; and I am watching over you tenderly, I am guiding you tenderly. As your Shepherd, I am tenderly watching over you. As your Father, I am caring for you and loving you and directing you. And I have ordained and planned that My will be done in your life here on Earth, as it is done, as it has been spoken, as it has been planned and ordained for you, in Heaven. All things in Heaven are done according to My plan and according to My will, and I am doing for you as I see fit and as I see is necessary to be done in your life at this time.

It is not an easy way that I take you, but it is a necessary way. It is the way to fruitfulness for you. It is a way of repentance, and it is a lowly, lowly way. I am bringing you

107

down, I will bring you down, to a very small, small kernel. I will bring you down to the size of a mustard seed that can be planted, so that you can die to yourself and come forth and spring up and blossom and be fruitful unto that which I have planned and ordained for you, My child. It is the way of smallness.

For those whom I will use greatly in My Kingdom will be made small. They will come to a place of weakness, where they feel that they can do nothing and that they are in such a straight place that they cannot move; they cannot go one way or the other. All they can do is look up unto Me, their Heavenly Father.

And that is where I have you, My child — in that place where you can do nothing but throw up your hands, as it were, even in despair, and say, "Now what do I do? I can't go this way, I can't go that way. This isn't working. I can't look back." All you can do is throw up your hands, My child. Lift them high unto Me and lift up your eyes unto Me, for I am the Alpha and the Omega, I am the Beginning and the End, I am the First and the Last. Look up unto Me, for I am all, I have all, and I will do all for you, My child.

I am working. I *am* working, but I will not thrust you out until I have done that work in your heart and in your life and in your mind that I have purposed to do. I am bringing all of you to a path and a place of humility — a lowly place where you realize that it is Me, and Me alone, in every area of your life. I will not use any of you until I have brought you down low, until you have fallen into the ground, until you have died to yourself — all of your wishes, all of your plans, all of your ambitions, all of your thoughts — and you let Me do as I please. Let Me, the Potter, do as I and only I know is right and best for you, for I have much for you to do; but it will not come about in the way you have thought or planned, for that is a way of the flesh.

There is so much flesh, so much flesh in this world and in

all of you, and it is a stench in My nostrils. And I am bringing you low, I am bringing you to a place of humility, I am bringing you to a place of love — such agape love for each other that you will esteem each other better than yourself; and you will not assert yourself, you will not put yourself above others, and you will not be hurt, if you are offended or stepped on or walked right into the ground! That is the place, My children, I am bringing you to, for I cannot use you until I bring you to that place.

And it is not an instant death; it is not instant, for My death on the Cross was not instant. I hung there for hours. And as I hung there, I suffered and I forgave. But I am calling all of you to that place of death — death to yourself and everything that pertains to you — so that you will humbly receive from My hand whatever comes. Whatever comes, you will humbly receive from My hand, without trying to figure out why, without saying, "I don't think this is right." Your thinking is getting in the way — in all of you! And I am bringing you to a place of humility, but it is the most blessed place that you have ever been in. You have not even begun to taste the blessedness of that place — of losing yourself, of dying to yourself, of giving your very life for those who are your friends and your servants and your loved ones. Giving your very life!

My child, let Me do this work in you. Let Me do it as the Potter. Let Me break you. Let Me make you again into another vessel, another vessel, fit and useful for My service.

And you, O My children, I have seen your tears, I have seen them. I have heard your crying, and I am answering your prayers, I am answering them; but you do not recognize it at this point. But know, My children, that I love you, I love you; and as your Abba Father, as your loving Heavenly Father, I do this work that only I can do. And all I ask is for you to yield and submit and to not fight it — to yield to these pricks, and not try to be something at this time that I'm not asking you to be.

All I ask you to do is to love Me with all of your heart and to love your neighbor as your very own self; and then you will be the pliable clay that I need in My hand to use and to work with at this time. I, your Father, am doing this work; and if it pleases Me (as the Potter) to call you and to let you (as the clay) rest, know that it is in this time when you feel like you're doing nothing, it is during this resting time, that I'm doing My specific and special work in you to make you more precious in My sight.

Do not fight it, do not fight it; but yield, yield, yield yourself unto Me. Lay down your own self, your own thinking, your own plans, your own wishes; and watch Me, your Heavenly Father, work and do this work that you would not believe even if it were told you, because that is the work I am doing now in these last and final hours.

No Death, No Resurrection, No Power

Do you really believe that I as your Father am working out all things for your good as you continue to seek Me with all of your heart? Do you really believe? Why then, when the hurt is deep and the pain intense, do you run into the arms of the flesh and depend on and draw from them, instead of staying with Me, enduring the pain and accepting the hurt as part of the process of death in your life to all that is not My will for you? Why do you find comfort in others' words when I have provided My words for you? Why do you look in despair for love other than Mine and trust others to bring wholeness to your spirit when I am the Healer of broken hearts and the Restorer of all things?

Do you not see that this thing is from Me? Do you not realize that in order to be acquainted with My suffering, you will experience loneliness, desertion, pain, and rejection? You stop short of death — death to your wants, desires, longings, choosings, ambitions, and plans. You hang between life and death. You sleep for sorrow and do not understand because of the hardness of your heart. Let Me be God in your life! Do not second-guess Me. The very thing you are rejecting and sorting out and putting in a slot for your own use and advantage, is the very thing I have planned for you. Lay all else aside and come, come to Me. I wait for you. I love you so much. It hurts Me to see you go this way of the flesh.

I am God; there is none else besides Me. My plan is good. Why do you fight it with your own thoughts and will? Why do you continue to set your heart on that which satisfies your fleshly needs, desires, and wants? The more you are willing to lay down your life, your thoughts, your plans, your desires, your hopes, and your dreams; and the more you recognize and realize that the path I am leading you on is not one that your flesh or natural reasoning mind would choose; then the more you will know the joy of being acquainted with Me in My sufferings, and you will be made conformable unto My death.

Surrender, surrender all! I'm asking for absolute surrender. Do not hang on to anyone or anything. Be as dead men to the things around you, and you will become alive unto Me. It is only as you die to yourself and all the things around you that I will be able to raise you up in power and newness of life to accomplish and fulfill My plan and purpose for your life. No death, no resurrection, no power! Set your heart to do My will, not yours, and thus fulfill and finish the work I have planned and ordained for you to do.

It is so important that you recognize the way I lead is not always easy. The laying down, letting go, cutting off, and cutting out of things will be painful, but I know the end from the beginning and from ancient times the things that are not yet done. My counsel shall stand; I will do all My pleasure. Do not fret, My child, only press in to the loving heart of your Father, who loves and cares for you, who shapes and molds you into the vessel He would choose. Do not be afraid. I am working out My great plan, and it shall be as I have spoken, but it shall not come about as you supposed. Trust Me that I am working out all things for your good.

I am teaching you invaluable lessons, hard lessons, but needful for you. I am breaking you and your will. I am working one way in your life right now and another way in others, but the end will be the same. Don't be afraid. Don't panic. It does not look now as it shall be. There are things that are not done yet, but I have spoken it. I will also bring it to pass. I have purposed it; I will also do it.

I Am Teaching You Lessons

My precious little children, My precious little children, do you not realize, do you not know and do you not call to your mind, do you not remember My Word, My Word to you which calls you, which calls you unto Myself and unto My heart, daily, hourly, every minute? I am calling and wooing and yearning and longing for you, My precious little children. Oh, I am teaching you lessons in this hour: lessons to make you strong, lessons to make you able to stand, lessons that will keep you from harm and injury in your life.

And, oh, you seem to feel like you are in such a tight place, in such a hard place. But know this, My children, know this, that the struggle in your life is in doing My will. That is the struggle that is going on in your heart and in your mind and in your circumstances right now — it is in doing My will. The struggle is to walk on the path that I am calling you to walk on. In the Garden did not My Son sweat, as it were, great drops of blood? What was the struggle about? It was in doing His Father's will, in doing My will. He said: "Not My will, but Yours be done." But there was that time when He said, "If it be possible, let this cup pass from Me. Nevertheless, Thy will be done." [see Matt. 26:39]

My children, I have placed you in certain circumstances, in strait places at this time. This thing is of Me, it is of Me: this hurt, this desperation, this desolation, this sickness. I have placed you there, My children. I am training you: I am training you to be good soldiers; I am training you to be strong in Me. Do not kick against the pricks. Just continue to come to Me, and know that I love you deeply. My love for you is so very deep that you cannot even begin to comprehend it.

Do not look around you, do not look behind you, do not even look ahead at this time. Look just to the step, the next step, that your foot will be on. Look to that, and do not project yourself; you will set yourself up for trouble if you do. Look to Me, the Author and the Finisher of your faith. Do you not know that I am the Alpha, I am the Omega? I am the Beginning, I am the End; I am the First, I am the Last. And what I do, I do in My plan, My great plan, and I do it for your good.

And I do it because I love you. I love you, I love you, I love you! Oh, if you could just hear it, if you could just hear Me loving you and hear My voice of love. If you would just let Me — allow Me — to place My arms around you. But you hurry so and you worry so, and you are so encumbered; and you think that I will not do right for you.

O My beloved little children, just come. Just come and kneel before Me; just come and sit with Me; just come and let Me hold you. Let Me embrace you; let Me comfort you. You need My comfort. Let My Holy Spirit, whom I have sent to comfort you, comfort you by My Word and by My Spirit. Let that comfort come to you — *allow it* to come to you. I have it for you.

I love you and I desire you. I need you and I want you.

113

You Are Weary in Your Wanderings

You are weary, My children, weary in your wanderings. And you are like the children of Israel. You are going around and around and around. You are thirsty, you are hungry, and you are weary. You are very weary in your wanderings. And you are wandering because you, like the children of Israel, do not believe that I am able to bring you out into the place where you desire to be. You have seen the grace, you have heard the report, and you know your God's ability to bring you out into that place; yet, because of fear and unbelief, you continue to wander in the wilderness.

When I say that I am the way, I am the truth, I am the light, and I am the life, and that I am able to bring you out and plant your feet in a place of fruitfulness, and yet you do not believe, then you are trusting and leaning to your own understanding. You lean to your own human reasoning, and you listen to an evil report; and you do not believe that I am able, your God is able, to bring you out.

I am desiring to bring you into a new place, into a new thing, and it does not only concern the things you have your eyes fastened on — it is much broader. It is of far greater expanse and proportion. And you are limiting yourself to a very small and a very narrow place and a place of death, really, where you will die if you do not believe that your God is able to bring you out into this new place, into a fruitful place. But it is different. It has a different flow, it has a different taste, it has a different smell. And part of it you have been refusing for many, many years, and you have not seen what I want to bring you into.

And so, My children, I want you to know that I love you; and in mercy I call you to get your eyes off the circumstances. Get your eyes off of what you see. Close your ears to the reports of what you hear, and look unto the Lord your God, and call to Him and cry to Him and seek Him and desire

Him. You have sighs in your hearts and in your voices and in your very being, but so do I.

And you read it in My Word, and I say, "Oh that men would praise Me for My goodness and for My wonderful works to the children of men!" [Psalm 107:8]. Do you not see it? You walk past the very thing that will bring you out, the very thing: calling on and remembering My mercy, and coming to Me and thanking Me for My goodness, and doing this in the midst of all these other things. When you cry out, when you cry out in the midst of these things, I will deliver you. I will send My Word. I will bring you out in the midst of your need, in the midst of your circumstance, whatever it is, My children, whatever it is.

It is a huge lesson, and you will remain where you are until you know that I, the Lord your God, am working a work and I am bringing you to a new place: a new place in Me, a new place in this age, a new place in this time. But it will only come as you realize that you cannot hold onto the old any longer, but you must release it, and step forth and break the ties and cut the strings so that you can go forth into this new place of fruitfulness for Me, this new place of life in abundance in Me, the Lord your God.

Lean Only On Me

Oh, My beloved children, My beloved children, do you not see, do you not sense the lesson that I am trying to teach you by My Spirit? Do you not know that it is not only necessary, but it's the most important lesson that I have to teach you? And in these Last Days and in these last hours it is the only lesson that you need to learn at this time. For it will take you from the place where you are into the depths of My heart and Spirit, and into the place that you long to be.

But it is so necessary, it is so important that you do not

lean upon anyone except Me, that you do not lean upon the arm of the flesh, that you do not depend upon the arm of the flesh or the words of the flesh or the comfort of the flesh or the desire of the flesh or the satisfaction of the flesh; but that at this time you lean on Me and lean on Me only. Because it is the bride who comes from the wilderness, the place of testing, the place of temptation — she comes out leaning on the arm of her Beloved.

And, My dearly beloved ones, this day I would have you know that it is the lesson of love that I am trying to bring home to you. And even though many parts of it may seem severe, know that the base of it is love, and that as you respond because you love Me — because you love Me — you will come to experience in your heart and in your mind and in your thoughts and in your feelings what you have never experienced before, and you will know that whatever comes, whatever goes, you can stand alone.

I said stand, My children. I said stand, leaning on Me. For if you do not, if you do not allow Me to bring you through, if you do not yield, if you do not let Me put this harness on you at this time, you will not stand! You will hold the hands of others. You will be comforted by them, but they will have to carry you. You will not stand. You will never stand through it all!

Do you see? Do you hear? Do you hear, My children? Do you comprehend? Do you perceive what I'm trying to work out within you? Do not resist; do not resist My love. For it is My love that calls you. It is My love that will teach you. It is My love that will hold you. It is My love that will bring you out, will bring you out victorious, will bring you out into the place that I desire for you, in the power of the Spirit of God. Jesus, My Son, came out of the wilderness in the power of the Spirit. Do you get it? Do you comprehend it? Do you know what I'm saying to you this day?

Continue to come to Me. Draw from Me all day long, all

night long. Want Me and Me alone with everything that's within your little hearts, and they will be enlarged. Enlarged and enlarged and enlarged! And from that place of death and dying to everything else will come what I have truly planned, what I have truly purposed for you and for the outworking and outcome of My Kingdom work in these last times.

You Asked to Share in My Sufferings

You said you wanted to share in My sufferings.

There was a continual suffering, a continual hurt, a continual grieving in My heart. I was a man of sorrows. I was acquainted with grief. I bore it. I was never really accepted for Who I really was or for what I had come to do. I loved freely and unreservedly but was despised and rejected. I was wanted and sought after for what I could give. My great love was spurned. In return I received superficial, self-seeking love.

You've asked to share in My sufferings. You've asked Me to unveil the Cross. Are you willing to bear it even if the end of that suffering is not in sight? Are you willing to suffer with Me even if the end is the most painful part of all according to what you can see in the natural? Are you willing to carry the cross, die on the cross, and flow mercy to all as the slow, painful, sorrowful death takes place?

You will only be able to accomplish this as you daily seek My face and are willing to let the Cross touch every area of your life. For it will only take place as you are willing to do My will in everything concerning you. The struggle of your will versus Mine will take place as you daily seek Me in a closet of prayer. That is where you will lay down your will — as you let Me search and try and know your heart, as you face your fleshly desires and lusts, and as you are willing to be broken and, in repentance, cry out for forgiveness and mercy. There will be no Cross without Gethsemane.

You asked to share in My sufferings. It will only happen as you die to yourself, which is basically your will. Out of that death you will be raised and transformed and conformed into My image, and with a truly merciful heart you will share in My suffering and grief over My Church and a world lost in sin.

You asked to share in My suffering. In participating in it you will first have to suffer the death of self, and then you will be able to share in My sufferings. Are you willing to bear this suffering for a season, until the appointed time?

The Place of Death

Who are you willing to be identified with — the rich, the lovely, the intellectual? Who will you choose to join yourself to? Of what reputation will you make yourself? What is your mind-set? How do you see yourself? What place or position are you striving for? Are you seeking to serve or be served? Are you seeking to minister unto Me or to others? If you choose to be truly identified with Me and My ways and My paths, then you must follow Me to the place of death and identify with Me there in humble submission to the will of the Father. It will mean a death to all that seeks identification with the things of this world, its lust and its pride.

Will you allow Me to do this necessary work in you? Will you give up and surrender all that you are identified with now? Will you be willing to be identified with Me in the agony and struggle of that death? Will you willingly submit to the path of death on the Cross? Will you be identified with Me, the Lamb of God, in submission, first of all? Will you be willing to be identified with Me as a lamb led to the slaughter, not opening its mouth? Will you bear reproach, hatred, mocking, scorn, and despisings? Or will you run from this path and be identified with those who put Me to death?

This is an hour of separation and identification. Only those who truly love Me with all their heart, mind, soul, and strength will be willing to bear this badge of identification, which is love — loyal, steadfast, faithful LOVE. I am looking for this loyal love that will lay down its very life to be identified with Me.

Do Something Significant for Me

Do you want to do something significant for Me? Fall into the ground and die! Do the insignificant things, the lowly things, the despised things. Let Me crack, break, and remove your outer shell of self. Suffer rebuke, scoffing, chastisement, blame, beating, and scorn. Respond in humility, meekness, mercy, and purity. Accept and forgive. Be laughed at, spit upon, ridiculed, and mocked. Love to the very end, and die. Be buried and look like you lost.

But wait. Something is stirring. A blade is coming up through the ground. Resurrection life is taking place! The dead seed is nowhere to be found.

Life Comes from Death

Early in the morning the women came, motivated and driven by love, to a tomb of death and separation, and found life. Eternal life had sprung forth. You too will find life in every death situation as you continually choose to follow and obey Me, whatever the cost.

Life only comes from death. Death will come to you in many shapes, forms, and sizes. Many times it will hurt and cause grief and pain. Do not be afraid. I lead you this way, but I am with you every step of the way. You will be misunderstood, judged, and criticized — many times. So was I. But only through death to yourself will you bring forth life

119

and fruit that will last.

Oh, do not be afraid to die. Do not be afraid to let go of all earthly ties. I lead you in a way you have not gone before, but I lead you. Remember that. There will be stops and starts, but there will be food and fellowship, nourishment, and watchful care. I will clearly point out areas that need to die. I will show you your unrighteous acts and deeds. I will surround you with My love and pour in the oil and wine to heal and restore you. Always My table is available to you. Always we have a "date" set to meet and be together for love and fellowship and intimacy. I will be there. I won't disappoint you, not ever! Do not disappoint Me.

Know that I love you deeply. I always have. Nothing you have ever done has made Me love you less. You are My precious, priceless jewel! I'm excited about this new year. Together we shall live and love. Together we shall pray and intercede. Listen for Me. Watch. Anticipate Me. Behold, I come, My beloved; I come, leaping upon the mountains, skipping upon the hills. I desire to be with you!

Depart from the Old

Some things are already done; they are finished. They no longer have to be thought about or planned for. In other areas, I have lifted the burden and moved you on to other things. Right now I am intensely working with you in the area of righteousness so that My character and image may be formed in you. There must be a departing from your old thoughts and ways and patterns. You must turn and forsake them. You must continue to cry out to Me to be broken. It is only as you surrender all, die to your self and its fleshly thoughts, cravings, and desires, that My life, light, character, and image can shine forth. There is still much to be broken. Keep coming, keep repenting and forsaking, as I reveal to you your foolish ways.

A New Day

It's time to start a new page. The old is finished; it is done. It's time to begin a new page — new happenings, new direction, a new day. Uncertainty and fear would be the norm for the carnal Christian. But I lead you on — on a path already planned for and predetermined. Fear not, I am with you, leading you each step of the way. It is a new day, a new time for you.

Walk carefully, follow Me closely. All the happenings of these past years have brought you to this very time and place. The past few months have brought you to a birthing of this very event. Rejoice! Look up, fear not! Walk carefully. There is still much you are holding onto that needs to be released. Many corrections and reproofs will bring you into the fullness of My plan and purpose for you. Walk carefully; there are many traps, snares, and gins laid out for you, to catch and entrap you.

I am teaching you the way of wisdom in all areas of your life. Obey Me, and do not be afraid or hesitate to act quickly on that which I command and show you. Much is at stake. Souls hang in the balance. Your obedience is imperative. Look not at what your natural eye can see. I am working on all fronts, in all areas, bringing to pass My plan, will, and purpose. It will not happen in the way you supposed, but it will happen.

Hold fast; cling tightly to Me. Cling and hold so tightly to Me that you will not be able to hold onto anything else. Let all else go! Let it fall by the wayside. Turn your face toward the wind and run — run toward Me and keep on running. Run to obtain the prize!

Even if I uproot and unplant you, I will plant you again. Set not your heart on things of this life. Set your eyes, heart, your affection, on Me, and Me alone. Desire Me above all else, and run and strive to obtain (win) Me. Watch for the new opportunities and the open doors. Examine each one closely. Walk carefully.

Continue to cry out to Me for direction. [see Psalm 25:4,5] It is a new way. I will lead you. Stay close, hold fast, cling tightly, and fear not.

The Bride is Being Prepared

I told you that I was arranging and rearranging. You are experiencing it in the natural. It is happening also in the Spirit. I am moving people to different areas. I am also sending people to different geographic locations, to assist in the arranging and rearranging. Many will stay only short periods of time, but they will assist in this arranging and rearranging, which has been needed for quite a while.

Part of this moving, shifting, and arranging has to do with cleansing, cleaning, and clearing. There is an order that will be the result of all that I'm doing now. The orderliness will be felt. It will be felt in the form of relief, the relief being in the accomplishment of doing that which has been needed for a long time. The order will also be felt in the cleansing and clearing. It will bring a sigh of relief — "Finally it is done, finally it is accomplished, finally it is in order." Keep in mind that this is all working towards the completion of My plan.

Remember this work is also being done in the Spirit. A great cleansing, purging work is being done. The bride is being prepared. This is the cleansing, preparation time. Every area of the bride's life will be touched by it. Only those who willingly and obediently submit, because of their great and passionate love for Me, will be thoroughly prepared for the Marriage Supper of the Lamb.

Listen, harken! Take heed to the Spirit's promptings. Yield yourself totally unto Me. Be pliable. Do not resist this vitally important work.

Come to the Quiet Place

I want you to be still in situations, as well as in times of sitting quietly before Me. The stillness of your spirit during times of stressful and hurtful and testing situations will be the result of a heart that has quieted itself daily before Me, in the secret chamber of prayer and in My Word. It is there in that place that I can teach and instruct you. It is there that I can show you the places of unrest and turmoil in your life. It is there that you will see the need for this death-to-the-flesh process I am taking you through.

It is only as you are willing to lay down your life to all that I reveal to you, that quietness and rest and peace and joy can come to your spirit — real rest, real peace, and real joy — My joy! It comes through humbling yourself and submitting to Me in every area of your life. It happens as you obey My command to love your neighbor as yourself, and as you are willing to lay down your life for them, esteeming them better than yourself in every situation. It is a death-to-self process that brings peace and quietness to your spirit. It is a work of the prayer closet that, in turn, is worked out in your everyday life situations.

It will take time. Keep coming. Once you have tasted of its sweetness, you will want to rid yourself of everything that destroys the quietness of your spirit. All else has a bitter taste and is filled with unrest and turmoil. Come, come to the quiet place and quiet yourself before Me. Be still and know that I am God.

Your thoughts and words need to be cleansed and purged and purified. If your heart is not quiet, your words will not be quiet. Quiet words come from a quiet heart — a heart free from pride, anger, bitterness, and moral impurity. Quiet words come from a heart of mercy.

Come, come and sit down before the still waters, and let

Me restore and refresh you. Come to the quiet place and quiet yourself before Me. Be still and know that I am God in every situation of your life.

Invite Me In

Invite Me in. Invite Me in. Ask Me to come into your garden to eat your pleasant fruit, and drink of your wine and milk. I'm waiting for you to invite Me in. The call of love is always two-fold: It's you answering My call of love to come and sup and fellowship and learn of Me; and it's Me responding to your call to come into your fragrant garden to eat your pleasant fruit and drink your wine and milk. Just as you want and desire Me to come and manifest Myself to you in your garden of love, so I desire and long and look for you to come to respond to My call of love.

I'm standing at the door. I'm looking through the lattice. Open to Me, My love, My dove, My fair one. Open to Me and come away to the secret place of the stairs. [see Song of Solomon 2:9-14] Invite Me in!

Let Love Grow

Let love grow. Love should always be a growing thing. It begins as a small seed planted in pure soil, the heart. It will grow and expand from the pureness of the soil, sun, rain, wind, and heat, and from the nourishment of the soil. The soil is actually hiding and cherishing the seed of love as it nourishes and stimulates growth. The condition of the soil to receive and keep the seed plays an important part.

The ear plays an important part. As you hear My voice, hear My Word, hear My call, and respond to My corrections and reproofs — as you sweat over them, as it were, as you remove the weeds and rocks, as you till the ground and make it soft and pliable — the planted seed of My Word will then grow. And love will also grow as you get to know Me and become acquainted with Me through times of repentance and brokenness and tears.

Hold nothing back. Let the light of the Word expose your heart. Be open and honest before Me. There are not only roots to be extracted, but there are rocks embedded in the soil that only the hammer of My Word can break. When all is finished, I will send My fire to devour them and burn them all up. They have hindered growth and fruitfulness.

Continue to dig in. There is much work to be done, many seeds to be planted.

Sharing

My children, I want you to know that as you share together, as you share back and forth, there is a bonding that takes place: a bonding in your hearts; and a bonding between you and Me, between you and the Father, and between you and the Holy Spirit. And there are two particular, specific things that also take place: one is that I record what you are saying — it is so very, very special to Me and that is why I record it — and also, what then takes place is what happened to the two on the road to Emmaus. As they talked about Me, as they talked about the things that had transpired, and after I joined Myself unto them and was invited into their presence, I revealed Myself unto them.

Do you see what happens, My children? You will be learning and you will be taught and you will be rejoicing My heart. Plus, I will be manifesting Myself, I will be revealing Myself to you in a very special way as you talk about Me, as you share about Me and My Word. These are such special, special times. They are more special than you know at this time.

Only as you press in to know Me, only as you continue on to talk and to share and to mull and to chew and to ponder — just to feel the specialness of these times — will you realize the work that is being done in your hearts and how very important and special this is to Me, and how much sharing is a part of this intimacy with Me that will grow and develop, as you talk and as you share. It's not just you and Me in your prayer closet. It is you and Me and the believers that I have joined you to. It's that talking also, and it's that sharing.

So know that this time with Me is very, very special. It is showing Me that you do love Me deeply. You love Me enough to put aside the fluff and all of the other things that the world might do, and you talk about Me. You talk about My Word and what you have learned and what you need to know and what you're hungry for and how what I've spoken is special to you. These times are very, very special to Me. They bear fruit. They are a time of growing. They are a time of learning. And you will know as the days go on, My children, and as you continue in this, how very important these times truly are to you and to Me.

Spend Every Day in My Courts[20]

"For a day in thy courts is better than a thousand. I had rather be a doorkeeper in the house of my God, than to dwell in the tents of wickedness." (Psalm 84:10)

One day in My presence is more precious than to live 1,000 days to one's self. It is not time that you need; it is **quality time**. The time that is spent in My presence is uplifting, healing, and restoring time. It lifts a person close to Heaven.

You do not need to go to a certain building to find this

"court of the Lord." Jesus told those who would listen that they would find it in their prayer closet. Every minute spent in fellowship and meditation in My presence is like a diamond compared to common baubles.

People do not know the worthwhileness of spending time in My presence. If they did, they would begrudge every minute that they spend frittered away in the affairs of this life. But I see few who find it hard to pull themselves away from My house and My presence. Most of them would rather do a million other things than enjoy the holy sanctity of My presence.

I want to fill you so full of My glory that your body can become the holy temple of the Lord, where My presence indwells your being at all times, so that even if you have to go about performing life's menial tasks, your soul will never be separated from the glory cloud.

Live every day of your life in the "court of the Lord." Never let a moment be wasted in idle prattle. Spend a lifetime in the courts of the Lord. It is possible to do this if you keep the door of your heart open to My indwelling presence.

All around you are the "tents of wickedness." Every ungodly and unholy life is a tent for wickedness to dwell in. Don't associate with these "tents." Separate yourself from their life-style. You must live in the world, but you do not need to become a part of this world. Separate yourself unto My holiness, and your life shall become a Holy of Holies, wherein My glory shall rest, causing every moment of your life to become a day of glory, a day in the presence of the Lord.

Only once a year, on the day of atonement, could the high priest enter My Holy of Holies, but you can live there all of your life in this High and Holy Place. Come! I'm waiting here for you!

I Am Drawing You to a Deep Love

My little child. I call you My little child, and I take you by your hand and I draw you to Myself. I turn you, I turn you to Myself. Turn your eyes toward Me. Look at Me. Look at Me, My little child. You are looking around. Sometimes you are looking at Me, but I want you to hold your gaze. I want you to hold your gaze as you look into My eyes.

You are Mine. You are My little child, My little child, and I desire you. I made you, I fashioned you, I formed you for Myself. And I desire you to be with Me. Not just to be with Me; I desire you to be *with* Me — with Me as I hold your hand and as I speak to you. I'm drawing your attention to Me. I want to hold your attention. I want you just to be held, enraptured, and enthralled as you gaze into My eyes; and I want you to know My love as you know no human love. I want you to know My love in that way, My child — a deep, deep love.

And I am drawing you to a deep love. And all the things that you think you can't do, all of the reasons that keep you from staying steady in My presence, all of those things . . . I will speak to you, I will teach you, and I will help you, as you grow to know Me more deeply; and you will know and come to the place where you will not want to look at anything else but Me. You will not want to look at any person or anything except Me. Continue, My child; fix your gaze and your eyes upon Me. I love you deeply. I love you dearly. I have chosen and called you to Myself, unto Myself, for Myself.

So do not worry or be concerned about other things at this time, for they shall come. And they shall all fall into place as you continue to come to Me and desire Me and fix your gaze upon Me, and Me alone. For I am jealous for you, My child, and I want you for Myself. I will teach you and train you in the way that you should go, and I will guide you with My eye. I will *guide* you with My eye.

So come, come, My little child, come to Me, and I will take you away and lead you the way that you should go. You need not fear. You need not fear, for I am with you all the way.

Look Into My Eyes

My children, I have something to say to you this day, something I want you to understand, and it is this: I want you to look into My eyes. Look into My eyes, My children. Do you not know that a lover longs to look into the eyes of his beloved? Do you not know that I am overcome with even one look of your eyes? And I want you to look into My eyes, but you do not come and look. You do not fix your gaze into My eyes. Fear — you do not do it because of fear. You do not do it because of busyness. You do not do it, in many instances, because you think you're not worthy. But the cry of My heart to you this day and the longing of My heart is that you would turn from the things you are looking at and look up. Look unto Me. Look into My eyes. Behold Me, behold Me, the One who loves you.

Do you not long to look into My eyes? Do you not long to stay steady long enough to look into My eyes and behold My beauty, to behold the great love and desire and longing that I have for you, so that I can whisper to you the things that I long to say to you? Do not be afraid of My love. Do not be afraid to tell Me of your love for Me. I long to hear those words. I long to hear you say that you love Me, that you desire Me. Come, My children. Come and look. Look into My eyes, and you will sense and you will feel and you will know the deep longing that I have for you.

Do you not see what you are doing as you come in to be with Me — that you are looking in the Spirit, as it were, at

all the things around you? You are thinking about all the
things pressing upon you, and so you rest in My love; but you
do not run after Me in the sense of looking into My eyes
—standing still, looking up and gazing into My eyes of love.
I am desiring that for you, My children. So come, come, look
at Me. Look at Me, and look into My eyes.

Heavenly Joy

My child, I want to give you My joy unspeakable and full
of glory. For My joy shall strengthen you, now and in the
coming dark days. You must live in the strength of My joy,
that which comes from intimacy with Me, from abiding in My
love. For fear has torment, but My love has joy. My joy
was always to bring joy to My Father, to do His will.

You anticipate the dark days to come and become morose
and fearful. You are not focused on Me! Why don't you fix
your heart, mind, soul, and eyes on Me? Listen, My child,
listen to what I say. Blessed with My life-joy are you when
men revile and persecute you and say evil against you falsely
for My sake. Rejoice and leap for joy, for great is your
reward in Heaven. When you are counted worthy to suffer
for Me and the sake of the Gospel, rejoice! When you bear
fruit for all eternity — souls for all eternity, whatever the cost,
and count not the cost — be joyful, for there is great joy in
Heaven over each soul that comes into the Kingdom. Spend
yourself, be spent for Me and for the saving of souls, for a
crown of joy awaits you. Remember, your affliction is light
and momentary here on earth, but the joy in Heaven is forevermore. And repentance from all sin is the way to a joyful
life, free from every sin that separates you from Me.

Where is your joy, My child? Look up to Me and lift up
your hands that hang down; lift up your voice and continuously
praise your God. Praise and worship Him with love songs

from your heart, your heart filled with love and thankfulness that you are a child of Almighty God. Then you will receive new songs, heavenly songs of the Spirit, to lift you heavenward. Gaze upon Me, instead of looking at television and the newspaper. Run to the Father! Run!

It was for the joy set before Me that I endured the Cross. Let that same joy lead you to deny yourself, My dear yokefellow, and go the way of the Cross. For only suffering releases resurrection life in you and through you to persevere to the end, to be faithful to the end. For suffering shall prepare My bride for My coming. If you avoid suffering, it will cost you your very life, now and forever!

Together, we shall accomplish great exploits as you delight to do your Heavenly Father's will and count not the cost. Let joy undergird your faith so you will come through these days of tribulation unto My appearing. Snatch every soul possible from the jaws of Hell!

Rise with your soul enraptured in Me. Live in Me. Let there be joy in the midst of sorrow, for the world must see in you My joy that doesn't depend on circumstances, but only depends on abiding in Me. Make Me your First Love, that I might make you an overcomer, even My bride. Pursue Me above all, for in My presence, moment by moment, shall My joy be in you and your joy be full.

Have you ever seen the radiant, heavenly joy on the face of one of My martyrs? If so, then you have beheld the glory of Heaven mirrored on the face of one who loves Me with all their heart and being. Perhaps one day I might see that glory on your face too, My child.

Songs of Love

Sing to Me, My children, sing to Me songs of love — songs of love to the Lover of your soul. Sing to Me songs from the love of your heart to My heart, for I long to hear your songs of love. I'm waiting to hear your songs — songs of love and adoration and praise, songs of thanksgiving, songs sung to Me from the very depths of your heart. Let them flow forth. Let these songs of love rise up from within your very being. Do not suppress them; do not hold them back, for they are waiting to come out — these songs of love, these phrases of love that you will sing to Me.

This is so much a part of the courting time between the bride and the Bridegroom: songs of love and adoration, songs that will rise up from your innermost being and express to Me the love thoughts that are in your heart. Let them come forth, My children. Let them come forth, for it is the time of singing; it's the time of the singing of the birds. It's the time of love. It's the time for the Song of Songs to be sung unto your Beloved from the depths of your heart and from a love that is deep and far-reaching — a love that is ever seeking out its love, a love that is ever seeking to be near and to draw close.

Those are the songs that I desire you to sing, and they will originate in the heart and mind of the bride, the one who loves deeply. They will come from the heart of the one whose first love causes her to sing songs to the One whom she so greatly desires. They are songs that are sung from a love that is *extravagant*, songs that are sung from a love that is *fervent*, songs that are sung from a love that is just boiling over with love and passion for her Loved One.

Sing them, My children. Sing to Me songs of love!

Seek Me First

The things you do today can have a far-reaching and eternal value — as you do them according to My plan, will, purpose, and calling. So do not let the things of this day consume you, but rather seek Me first and sup and fellowship with Me all day. Delight yourself in Me; take great pleasure in Me. Be thankful and excited about all My love thoughts and words and actions toward you this day. Know that I love you deeply. You bring great pleasure to My heart, My sweet one. Press in closely, and don't forget our quiet times together. They are the most special of all. I am *always* waiting for you.

Come Away with Me

Come away, come away with Me, and learn the lessons of love. Come away and learn to love Me. Come away with a heart willing to be entirely Mine. Come away and learn all about Me. Come away into the wilderness, where you will learn to be totally Mine, dependent and leaning on Me and Me alone. I want you to be a garden enclosed — MY garden enclosed — a beautiful fragrant garden. Come away and learn to be content and satisfied with My love and Mine alone. Your heart is still longing and yearning and pining for love other than Mine. Come away with Me. I long for you. I wait for you.

5. Intercessory Prayer

The Bride in Action (I)

*As the bride-in-preparation is seeking God
and getting to know Him more intimately, she can
begin to pray the burdens close to the Lord's heart.
The more she prays those burdens, the more she is
preparing her heart to be the bride of Christ.*

The Mover of My Unseen Hand

This harvest is the work of the unseen hand that writes on the hearts of men. Prayer is the mover of My unseen hand. Fear not the work of prayer because you do not see results in this world. Have faith in Me. Follow Me along the unseen path of prayer, for it leads through the dirty, dark, miry places and into the darkest of hearts, and it picks people up with the Shepherd's hands and carries them in His arms to Heaven, the home of our eternal presence. Be free in My Spirit. Be free to pick up and go to prayer whenever I say, "Come!"

Why Don't You Pray?

Why don't you pray, My children, why don't you pray? The reason man doesn't pray is because his mind tells him it is foolishness. Yes, the battle is in the mind. Only with the heart can man believe. Only with the heart will man believe and receive the things of God — that prayer will and does accomplish great and mighty purposes of God. In the natural man, in his mind, they are foolishness. Why don't you believe with your heart, My children?

Only those who spend much time with Me, in My presence, come to believe with their hearts the truth of the power of prayer. That's why only those who deeply love Me and spend much time with Me in the secret closet, with the door closed, believe in prayer. Only as we spend much intimate time together, can I open your hearts and eyes to this Truth. As your hearts are knit together with Me and you believe with your heart, then the desire to pray and a love to pray and the reality of the power of prayer will come to you and take hold in your life. Then as you pray, you will know that prayer moves mountains out of the way, binds unseen spirits and cancels their assignments, and breaks down strongholds — all so that the arm of God can save. The unseen power of prayer makes the way for the Great Shepherd to pick up lost sheep on His shoulders and carry them to safety.

This is the truth, the great Truth, that many of My children read in the Word and speak forth with their mouths, but in their hearts they don't really believe. Their hearts are far from Me: not filled with My love, not My dwelling place, not My sanctuary, not totally yielded to Me.

It is only as you believe deeply in your heart, ablaze with My fire of love for you and for the souls of men, that prayer is that mightiest of powers from Heaven to move upon the earth . . . only then will you pray with fervent, heartfelt, effectual, rescuing, bondage-breaking power by the Spirit to establish My Kingdom on Earth, as it is in Heaven.

Why Do My People Not Pray?

Oh, why, oh why, do My people not believe in the power of prayer? They talk about it, they teach about it, but why do My people not pray? Why? Why don't you, My people, believe that which I say, that which I have shown in My Word, that which I have shown even in your own land, even in generations past, and today in many unexpected places around the earth — that prayer is the power through My people to accomplish My purposes in the earth? Oh, it grieves Me, it grieves Me so!

It is because your hearts are not knit together with Mine. It is because you don't really know Me. It is because you won't go into that secret place of prayer with Me because you don't want to be hidden away with Me. You want to be where man sees you; it is that spirit of pride that wants to be seen by man.

But, My beloved, I say, if you will come away with Me, if you will come into that closet of prayer, if you will gather together in My presence where I am in your midst, I will lead you into the mighty work of prayer for My purposes in these Last Days.

Oh, My people, I beg you, I cry out to you, will you pray? Will you ask Me to teach you to pray? Will you ask the Spirit to pray through you? Will you give up yourselves and humble yourselves and ask Me to show you how to pray? For I will not withhold it.

True prayer is a work, a labor, that takes much of spirit, soul, and body. True fervent, effectual prayer will cost you much; it will cost you much, and there will be no glory from man, but it will glorify Me. It will bring in that which I so desire to do in these Last Days; it will bring down the rain, that revival rain from Heaven, in and through a people. It will come in and through a people who will pray and pray!

Oh, I say, break through! Break through and hear Me call you to pray. Give up everything that stands in the way and come to Me, and I will teach you. It's the one thing that My disciples asked for. They said: "Lord, teach us to pray." They learned that it was the thing they had such need of. And by the power of the Holy Spirit in you, those things that stand in the way will be removed, burned out, cut away, and uprooted, in order that I might accomplish great things, things that you have never dreamed of. But you must let Me have My way, to break you. And you must give yourself to Me unequivocally, totally, without any strings attached, that I might have My way, that My power might be loosed through My intercessors.

Oh, My people, pray! Let go of everything else, and seek Me in the closet, even in the secret closet of prayer, and see if you will not go out from My presence in the power of My might to pray those fervent, effectual prayers that will accomplish My purposes, My will in the earth.

The Call to Deeper Intercession

These are perilous times, and I have called you to walk uprightly before Me. In the midst of adversity you must grow stronger in Me, and that comes through daily communion with Me. I am calling you to a deeper level of intercession, for there are not many who will answer the call. There are many who will serve in other capacities, but not many who will be watchmen on the walls. This is why I need you home. Your prayers are effective both for your personal petitions and for the nation and the world. As you pray and as you praise and worship Me, strongholds are being torn down, and more ground is being won for the Kingdom of God. Has that not been your cry — to do something that mattered in the Kingdom, that would further the Kingdom of God?

Not many answer this call to prayer, and not many really want to give of themselves to Me in the way that is necessary for My purposes to prevail. And prevail they shall, saith the Lord of Hosts. I have an Army. I have a remnant of prayer warriors, of people called by My Name, who seek no glory themselves and are willing to be separated in order to do My will.

You are right, that I call you to worship Me — to be a worshipper — but I need intercessors now like never before. The two go hand in hand. You cannot separate them. There is no conflict, for I am the Lord who calls you to know My heart. When you know My heart, you both worship and intercede. I will be glorified and My plans will prevail, saith God. Go now in peace, and accomplish the tasks of the day to please both your family and your God.

Surrender All that You Are, to Me

My child, surrender ALL — all that you are, all that you shall be, all that you want in your life, all that you do not want to be in your life — to Me. Is there anything left for you? Is there honor yet to be gained among men? Is there glory to call your own? Is there love from your family and your friends that goes first to you before it goes to Me? What and how much love and loyalty and help are you asking of church people and family? Are you asking others for what must come from Me and Me alone? Do you leave the choice to Me whom I will use to bring to you the necessities of the flesh and the love your spirit and soul need for nourishment?

Do you love the Lord your God above all others? Will you give Me the gift of your life that I have given you? Will you give to Me the hours and minutes of your day most precious to you? Will you stop striving? Do you truly believe My Word that I, and I alone, will and can fill you to overflowing abundance with all your life-needs? Yes! Yes! I can and will fill you with abundant life that only I can, and will, and do give to those who love Me above all others!

I, the Christ, the Messiah, am your Lord, and I ask if you will make Me your Master; and will you be a willing hand for My arm, a willing heart to cry My tears, willing eyes to see My world as I reveal it, willing ears to hear the cries of the lost little fish drowning in the sea of iniquity, and a willing tongue and lips to teach and preach My love and Salvation Plan? — to the ones the world calls ugly, gross, crippled, and sick in mind and heart, and the dirty "smelly" ones, whom I love with all that I am, who will come in from the garbage-littered streets and alleys to My banquet hall.

My banquet hall will have the most lovely table settings and sumptuous foods to feed the hungry, dying, crying-out-to-Me, lost fish in the sea, about to go over the edge to their everlasting doom. Come with Me, My beloved. Together we will rescue those who are torn and bloody and confused, lying in the ditch by the side of the road. I have come to heal their broken hearts, their broken, sick bodies, and to deliver them from their tormented minds, to set the captives free — free to know Me and love Me and serve Me, in love and in truth.

By My Spirit, My Holy Spirit, will I lead you into the path of righteous service unto Me. For I have chosen you to come and lay your burdens down at My feet and never pick them up again. I have chosen you to be My intimate companion through prayer. I will lead you and teach you and, yes, I will give you strength, determination, and perseverance to be My intercessor for the lost (the lost who will be found through your intercession). You will stand in the gap. You will be a repairer of the breach in the wall that will keep the lost from going over the edge into the Abyss. The current toward Hell and damnation is strong in the gap that I have placed you to fill. But by total dependence — total surrender of all that you are and ever could be, to Me — you will fill that gap. Yes, the ravens will feed you, and the angels will hold up your arms, as you stand tall and strong in My armor with My Word as your offensive weapon and with your feet upon the Rock.

It is a lonely gap I have called you to. Only I and My Spirit and My Son will be your Companions. Those on shore will point the finger and ridicule and mock. But your eyes, the eyes of your mended heart, will see only those who are desperate for My Love and My Salvation. Call unto Me! Seek Me first above all your needs and wants, and I will be found by you and by the many you fill the gap for.

Sound the alarm, for My Holy Army is on the march! Fear not, fear not, for I AM is with you, upholding you with My strong right arm — always! I shall never leave you. In the heat of battle I am by your side, a rear guard and a light to your path. Lean on Me, My bride, lean on Me alone.

The Highest Form of Prayer

Do you realize, My children, the wealth of treasure that you have at your disposal? The gift of the Holy Spirit imparted to you from the Father is immeasurable in value. Do you realize how valuable and important this gift is to you at all times? Do not take it lightly. Esteem it highly.

Praying in the Holy Ghost is the highest form of prayer. It takes you out of the natural realm of human, natural thinking and reasoning, into praying the will of the Father. How important and necessary and invaluable is this kind of prayer to you. It covers all bases. The Holy Spirit knows the mind and will of the Father for every situation and need. He will lead you into all truth as you pray. Yield to Him. Ask for His help and guidance, and believe that He is leading and directing you.

Much prayer is needed at this time. It is an urgent hour! The judgment of God is about to fall! There is no way you can pray without the Holy Spirit's help. There is no way in the natural that you can pray for the things coming upon this land, without divine help and enabling. The Holy Spirit Himself will alert you to pray ahead of time for impending judgments and needs that are surfacing.

The hour is late; the needs are great. The time is one of urgency! Call on the Holy Spirit for His help. He will help you pray the deep things of My heart. Cry out! Be available. Lay other things aside. I call you to this Holy Ghost praying. Yield yourself and appreciate this great gift. Pray in the Holy Ghost!

Praying in Tongues[21]

Speak the language of My Spirit unto Me morning and evening. It is more powerful than your other prayers alone. It will add to thee many things, including depth of Spirit worship.

It is not always important that you understand (to feed your intellect*). I understand, and is that not the point of praying? The Spirit helps you pray that which cannot be put into words by your intellect, makes intercession unto God for others, and even supplicates for thyself.

Speak the language of My Spirit that I have given you, and you will find it a great help to your walk. You have avoided it because you did not see the point in praying in such a way that could not be understood by you, but that is not what tongues or Spirit language is all about. It is Holy Spirit intercession unto God: He prays through you, concerning you and also concerning others. Therefore, lift up holy hands and pray in the Spirit every day, and you will see your progress change and go even faster, saith the Lord.

So, speak to Me in My Spirit language. . . . This is what you need to use if imprisoned and unable to write, or if you don't know what to pray. This prayer comes unto Me in My Kingdom, regardless. It isn't for you or anyone to take lightly. You thought you only use it before people as evidence of the Holy Spirit in your life, but this is not so, for Paul said, "I thank my God that I speak in tongues more than you all. I pray with the Spirit and with the understanding also." [see I Cor. 14:18,15a] Paul also sang in the Spirit and with his understanding. Yes, I know your reasons — that this is a lonely walk, and understanding thy own prayers edifies the natural mind, where Holy Spirit prayer does not — but Spirit intercession helps much more than this. You cannot know how much more.

*mind

142

Why Tongues?[22]

It is a way of speaking through My people. It tenderizes the soul of the one who speaks and of the one who hears. It is My "foolishness" that confounds the proud, the unbeliever; for therein the heart of God can touch the one who seeks His fullness.

It bows down the egotistical, the arrogant, and lifts up those who feel beaten down. All are in need of the fire that cleanses the dross and chaff of life, the unfruitful and empty efforts of man.

My things of power come through the anointing by My Holy Spirit. "Tongues" is the prayer of praise in the Spirit, the overflow of love in the Spirit.

[The person who received the prophecy speaking]: "Tongues is God's 'cleverness' to put all under one level of communication with Him. It is a vehicle of expressing the heart of praise to God. The proud one, the fearful, the calloused culprit, the tearful mourner — all praise the Father in one mode, one level of prayer."

"It releases pent-up, unexpressed feelings. It expands the heart. It edifies the soul. 'The foolishness of God is wiser than men' is once again exemplified here."

[God speaking]: The tongue that praises Me is tender to My Spirit. Blessings come to the heart that worships Me in this way. I direct your tongue into intercessions also for those who are needing prayers said for them.

Forsake Not
The Fountain of Living Waters within You[23]

.... If, when you glorify Jesus, you will praise Him from the depths of your heart, many of you will find that your wells need to spring up, as Moses spoke to the children of Israel and they cried, "Spring up, O well, spring up." You can cry out to the wells of living water in you, which sometimes become stale and silent, because I would have them to move. I would have them moving in other languages to come from deep within you, because I have installed wells of living water within My people who have spoken in other languages — even in other tongues, as they did on the Day of Pentecost and as they did throughout the epistles in the Scriptures. Beware, therefore, lest ye be decoys and allured with mental powers and forsake the fountain of living waters. For I have said I will never leave you nor forsake you.

There remaineth a rest to the people of God, and this rest is magnified by the words of Isaiah in the 28th chapter. Read there the words he spoke: "Whom shall He teach knowledge? And whom shall He make to understand doctrine? Them that are weaned from the milk and drawn from the breasts. For precept must be upon precept, precept upon precept; line upon line, line upon line; here a little and there a little: For with stammering lips and another tongue will He speak to this people, to whom He said, This is the rest . . . and this is the refreshing; yet they would not hear." [see verses 9-12]

These are those days when men are restless and cannot sleep, neither can they rest in their ministries and activities, because of the lack of the rest in their souls and in their spirits. I have offered them the fountain of living waters. I have offered them wells of living waters, springing up into everlasting life. My servant Paul in the 14th chapter of First Corinthians made reference to Isaiah's prophecy when he said, "In the law it is written, With men of other tongues and other

144

lips will I speak unto this people; and yet for all that will they not hear Me, saith the Lord."

How many have grieved My Holy Spirit by veiling, yes, putting a veil over the Pentecostal truth. When I hear My servants preach and put a veil over that speaking in heavenly languages, My heart is grieved and I am vexed with this.

But you who know Me in the power of the baptism of the Holy Spirit, evidenced by speaking in other languages, know the joy and the glory and the wells of living water within you. Oh hear My voice tenderly calling to you today. Come unto Me all ye that labor and are heavy laden, and I will give you rest. Yes, I want you to come to Me now as you read these words.

Turn back to the 14th chapter of First Corinthians and behold the joy of the believer who speaks forth in another language, who speaks triumphantly to the church and to the people, to the congregations and sometimes to Me, saith the Lord, where no one understands that communication between Me and the soul; and the devil himself knoweth it not. Sometimes some of My servants pray and praise Me until they are raptured into a great place; yes, transfixed ascendancy. It is the joy of their soul to speak for hours in intercession or communion, communication or the power of the Lord within them to heal them, to answer their questions. This is the Holy Spirit that maketh intercession with groanings that cannot be uttered. But there is an utterance that My people have that should be known. Fear has sometimes engulfed their joy and has stifled them. It has muffled their mouths.

Come unto Me, My people, and repent of this thy ignorance. For I would not have you to be ignorant, my brethren, said Paul. I would have you to come to Me, the Lord Jesus. For I am within you and you are within Me, and I am the Lord thy God that leadeth thee in the way that thou should go.

Stand in the Gap

If you will take fasting times and zero in on a particular need and lift that need up to Me and believe that as you seek Me concerning it, that I will hear and answer according to My great plan and design, you will see much accomplished and brought to pass. Be willing to stand in the gap. Be willing to intercede for peoples and lands and nations and for the cleansing of the Church, which is so necessary and urgent at this time.

Great darkness is coming on the face of the earth — trouble and persecution, a great falling away! Those not anchored fast to the Rock of Ages will fall away! Those not planted and firmly rooted in Me will follow their own hearts' desires. Many will become offended because of Me and My Word and will choose the easy way, the broad way. But those who love not their lives unto the death, those whose heart is wholly Mine, will be as burning, shining lights.

Ask for Souls![24]

Yea, and this year thou shalt ask for souls. Ask for souls! Ask for souls! Do not ask for things . . . ask for souls!

The Bride Will Meet Her Bridegroom in the Harvest Field of Prayer

Yea, I say unto thee, covet souls, My children; covet not kingdoms of this world, but covet souls. Ask of Me, that thy garners might be full of souls from the Lord; yea, that thy quiver might be full of children, saith the Lord thy God. For I want to bring in a great harvest. Yea, the day of harvest has begun. Yea, I have put the sickle into thy hand, My child, and have entrusted thee to go and bring in the harvest. And I say unto thee, even as Ruth came to Bethlehem for the time of harvest, so thou hast come even unto this time and place, and it is thy "Bethlehem;" and here thou shalt have a great harvest. For this is thy Bethlehem, and this is thy House of Bread, and this is thy time of harvesting.

Yea, as thou art even in the fields of harvest, even as thou art gathering in souls, thy "Boaz" (Jesus, thy Redeemer) shall come. Yea, in the time of harvest He shall come, and He shall choose you as His bride, as Boaz chose Ruth. For I say unto thee that the Lord of the Harvest will not look for His bride on beds of ease, comfort, and luxury, but the Lord shall look for her in the harvest field. There is where He shall find her and take her to Himself. . . .

Sigh and Cry with Me

Come, My children, come and sigh with Me. Sigh and cry over the sins and abominations of My people. Come, come and sigh, for their sins are many, their wound is deep, and their sins are incurable. They do, everyone, that which is right in their own eyes. They are slidden back with a perpetual backsliding, and they do not know the depth of their backslidings. Oh come, My children, come. Come and sigh with Me. I am looking for those who will sigh and who will cry over the sins and the abominations of My people.

Just as Jesus wept over Jerusalem, so you, My people, must weep over your city and over your church. You must weep with compassion and grief over a people who will not repent, who will not turn from their wicked ways so I can heal their land. Weep for a people who have ears but do not hear the voice of the Spirit. Weep for a people who have eyes but do not see the things of the Spirit. Weep for a people who are overcome with the cares of this life. Weep for a people who sow, but not unto Me. They shall reap a whirlwind! They have little or no understanding of the ways of the Spirit, for they seek Me not. I will be found of those who diligently seek Me. I will be found of those who hunger and thirst after Me. *They* shall be filled.

Weep

Weep, O My children, for as you weep, the angels gather those tears in censers and send the power of those tears upon My people and upon the lost of this generation to break bondages, hindrances, and that hardness of heart and blindness of mind that keeps them from Me.

You don't understand the power of weeping and travailing, but simply know it is My power in a vessel abandoned to Me, filled with My Spirit. It is from them that My Living Waters flow. As you weep, My life-giving and bondage-breaking Blood flows, and My anointing breaks yokes. I have ordained it that way.

Those who truly seek the Spirit of Prayer will receive the Spirit of weeping and travailing, if they persevere until I rain down that anointing from Heaven. For it is your tears that distill the rain from Heaven as you rend your hearts and cry out to Me. When you weep, you are one with Me, for I, too, am weeping. And that weeping holds back the final judgment for a season.

Oh weep, My children, weep for the slain of the daughter of My people, for the lost of the world, for the backslidden, and for the hardest sinners, that many may come into My Kingdom. Let your tears flow as mighty rivers to the desert places of humanity where I desire to bring forth My Life, even in those who appear to be dead!

Now is the Time to Travail and Bring Forth

You will need to walk very carefully in these last and closing hours. As the last and final call is being given, the forces of the enemy are doubling their efforts to catch you off guard, to trip you up, to steal from you your precious and priceless moments with Me. All is in readiness in the heavenlies. I await My Father's command to go and take My bride unto Myself.

Who will I find that will be found faithful? Who will be earnestly and lovingly looking for and expecting Me? The time is short. There is much to be accomplished. I need My faithful bride to be ever awake and alert. I need for her to heed My call and to separate herself and close herself in with Me. I need her to meet with Me on a moment's notice in her secret closet of prayer. I need her to weep with Me; I need her to cry and pray and groan and travail. I need her to bring to birth that which is ready to be birthed.

Guard your heart. Watch and pray. As you respond to My leadings, you will find yourself praying in a way you have never experienced before. The hour is late and now is the time; now is the time for you to travail and bring forth. Do not take this casually. Self-centered interests will cause you to attend to other things and abort that which is heavy and ready to come forth. Watch; walk carefully. Separate yourselves and yield yourselves totally unto Me. I need you.

The Hour of Birthing is Come

My children, I want you to know this day, and I want to assure your hearts, that I love you. My love for you is so deep, so deep! The love I have for you is a love beyond any love that you have ever felt or seen or experienced or can even comprehend up to this present time. I love you with a love that is ever calling, a love that is ever calling and wooing you to My heart, to come close to My heart. And I know you, My children, that you are responding; and I do need you to respond and do My will — to take up your cross at this time and follow Me and do My will. I will strengthen and I will help and I will undergird you in all areas.

Do not be afraid to do My will. Do not be afraid to submit yourself and to surrender yourself to do My will at this time. It is so important that you listen and obey. It is so important. It is *imperative* that you listen and obey. Continue to come, continue to love Me, continue to cast aside and lay aside everything that would hold you back from coming. Lay down those things that I am talking to you about. Set them aside, turn from them, and continue to come to Me. Continue to come.

The need on My heart is great at this time. The need is so great, and it is heavy on My heart. For the birthing time, the time to bring forth, is now. And I need you to be in the place of birthing. I need you to be aware that that is what it is. I need you to be alert to the time and the hour, for the hour is come, the hour of birthing.

If you do not yield to My love, if you choose not to — if you choose to satisfy your own lusts and desires and pleasures and feelings — you will abort that which I have placed within you. You will abort it! You will actually kill the thing that I am wanting you to bring forth and the thing that I am wanting to bring life to.

The choice is yours today, My children, the choice is yours. And I bring it to you in love, knowing that because you love Me, you will choose My way. But know that it is important; it is so very important! Many other things will call to you. Many other things will seem right according to your natural human reasoning and even according to the way you have been doing some of them up to this point, but you must know that I call, I call in love. And I will direct you, I will help you, as you yield yourself in love to this call.

Do not be afraid. It shall not be as you think. So do not be afraid, and do not hold back. Do not hold back. Yield, yield to My tender love. Yield to My mercy call of love to your heart, for I love you. I love you, and I've chosen you for this specific time and task. I love you, My children.

The Harvest is Waiting
Where Are the Intercessors?[25]

by Gwen R. Shaw

"No one can come to Me unless the Father . . . draws him." (see John 6:44)

Man is totally at the mercy of God, but he doesn't realize it. He thinks (and sometimes even we think also) that he can come to God whenever he desires to do it. But this is impossible. It is only by the grace of God that we can come to Jesus. It is only by the grace of God that any Jew can believe that Yeshua is his Messiah. No man can come to Jesus unless the Father invites him to come.

Intercession Brings the Souls to Birth

That is why intercessory prayer is so vital for the salvation of souls. It takes the physical travail of the mother for anyone to be born into this natural life. And it takes spiritual travail of the spiritual "mothers of Israel" for anyone to be born into the Kingdom of God. That is why Paul said to the Galatians, "My dear children, I am suffering the pains of giving birth to you all over again; and this will go on until the Messiah takes shape in you." (Galatians 4:19)*

The reason we have "church growth" instead of revival is because there is not enough true travailing of the Spirit. The Church is giving "dry birth" to "still-born babies." There

151

is no life in them. They have not been truly born again. They are "still born." There is no sound in them, no motion, no feeling coming from them, because they are without life. And all our fleshly efforts are in vain. We need revival!

We need to cry out to God from the depths of our souls that the Father will call sinners to Jesus and the Jews to their Yeshua. It will take a miracle. *We have lived so long without miracles in the Church that we have grown accustomed to their absence!* We have managed so well to produce "fire on the altar" without praying it down, that we think we can also manipulate, advertise, and manufacture a revival. But we are deceiving ourselves. It is time to fall on our faces and cry aloud and spare not, like a woman in travail.

Pain-Killers Will Hinder Spiritual Travail

So many women, when they are in travail, are given pain-killers and anesthetics to ease the pain. The "intercessors" of the Church are the same. They do not want to suffer the pangs of spiritual childbirth. They want their revival without feeling any agony of the soul for the lost. We are so accustomed to pain-killing drugs that we refuse to suffer in spiritual warfare. God help us!

Jesus is coming soon! And we are not ready! So many are still lost! If we do not cry out to God and allow His Holy Spirit to use us in travail, we will lose this harvest! Then how can we stand before God when all we have to bring Him is our hours of work for the Church? It is not "church works" that God needs now, it is travail in the Spirit!

Let it not be said of this Church-generation, "The children are come to birth, and there is not strength to bring forth." (see Isaiah 37:3b) Nor may the Church have to confess, when the time to give birth comes, that "We have been with child, we have been in pain, [but] we have brought forth wind; we have not wrought any deliverance in the earth. . . ." (see Isaiah 26:18)

152

Remember the words of Jesus one more time: "No man can come to Me, except the Father draws him."

Maybe you have never "travailed through" for that husband, that wife, that son or that daughter! It is possible that while you have been praying all these years for that loved one's conversion and you have, in grief, seen him run from God, that you yourself have sought to escape the "delivery room" — where all births take place — even the altar of travail for souls. Think about it. Be honest with your soul today.

It is time to travail for our children! Too many are lost!

*Jewish New Testament

Who is Willing
To Go to the Place of Birthing?

You are satisfied to sit around and hear preaching and read books and be stirred and moved, even to tears at times, but who is willing to go to the place of birthing and anguish and agony of soul? Who is willing to return to the place of prayer day after day to pour out their soul and cry out for the lost and the needs of others? — not at their convenience or choosing, and not according to their mind-set or pattern or tradition or learning. Who is willing to lay it all down and go for it — throw caution to the wind and give themselves unreservedly?

[The person who received the prophecy speaking]: "We are all so preoccupied with our own thoughts and ways and imaginations. We are full of ourselves and our own thinking, our own needs and wants and desires. We are full of our own human reasonings and conclusions, full of our own fears and plans, full of our own understanding. Full, we are full!"

[God speaking]: Just as all the inns were full and overcrowded at the time of My Son's birth here on Earth, so you are full, and you do not even recognize My voice knocking and wanting and requesting to come in. You do not sense the urgency. A baby is about to be born. Time is running out! You are preoccupied and taken up with the cares of the day. You are full, full to the brim. No more room. You miss your greatest opportunity!

The Cry of the Lost

Oh, do you not hear it, My children? Do you not hear it? Do you not hear the cry of the lost? Do you not hear the cry coming from the innermost being of those held in captivity and bondage? It is a sorrowful cry, it is a desperate cry, it is a hopeless cry.

They cry by reason of their bondage. Do you not hear their cry? It is coming up into the ears of the Lord of Sabaoth. It is a continuous cry. Do you not hear it? It is sounding out, it is ringing out, it is crying out! But you do not hear it. You do not care to hear it. It would disrupt your everyday, busy, self-centered activities!

Oh, how My heart bleeds, how My heart grieves. I call for intercessors; I look for them, but I find none. None that will really care, that will continue to share and bear with Me that burden that is continuously on My heart.

Listen, My children, listen. Not just for your own gain. Listen to the cry. Respond to the pleading. Stand in the gap for a nation that is crying for help!

Mournful Cry

Mournful cry — how will you respond to it? Will you reason it out? Will you feel it out? Will you respond to it according to your feelings? Will you give it time? Will you give it place? Will you take it and pray, by faith? Will you pray for what you cannot see or feel at this time, acting solely on the fact that I have alerted you to the need of the lost, who cry mournfully, continuously, without stop? How will you respond? Your choice and decision will mean Heaven or Hell! Your choice will affect eternity!

I Long to Share My Burdens with You

You, My children, have set your hearts and minds on Me to love and worship Me with all of your hearts. I have taken you through times of testing to prove what is really in your heart and to show you areas not yet yielded to Me. Keep coming, keep desiring, keep responding to My wooing. Keep examining your heart. Keep listening and obeying My reproofs and corrections. I am bringing you into a plan of union: one in heart, thought, and purpose.

How My heart longs for you, to have you near, sitting and listening as I pour out to you the burden on My heart, as I share with you, as I open your eyes to see as I see — to see the hurt, the lonely, the desperate, to see and feel the cry of the lost. Oh, how My heart longs to be with you. Oh, that you would have time for Me. Oh, that you would recognize what I show you. Oh, that you would be willing to weep with Me over what I lay on your heart. Oh, if only you'd take time as Mary did, removing yourself from the duties of the day to fellowship with Me, to join with Me only because you love Me deeply and desire Me and want to acquaint yourself with Me.

I want to be your Lover. I want to share with you as lovers do. Oh, that you would listen as lovers do. I long, I *long* to tell you the burdens on My heart. Oh, that you would respond as a lover would, eager to join with Me in suffering, eager to bear it till the deliverance is wrought. I love you deeply and long to share My burdens with you.

You Do Not Understand About My Burdens[26]

You do not yet understand, My children. Do you not understand that you are like the disciples who came and wanted explanations, but it was because of the hardness of their hearts that they did not understand? And this morning I perceive that you do not understand about My burdens. You do not understand about the burden for the lost. And I do not say this to condemn you, but I speak this as an instruction and a help to you — to encourage you to come and to know and to perceive and to understand the burden for the lost and the burden for the Church in these last and final hours.

Look at My life. Read it, and look and see in My Word how I said that I was One with the Father, and that I always did those things that pleased Him. And it was because of this that He could share with Me the deep burdens on His heart. For you will not be able to bear the burden that is on My heart unless you are one with Me.

Have you not heard Me say time and time again, have I not called and called for you to come with ALL of your heart, to come with all of your heart and to lay down the things that would hinder you and keep you from knowing Me deeply and intimately? For as you come I will be able to trust you; I will be able to share with you those things that are on My heart.

For the cries of the lost are coming up even now unto the ears of the Lord of Sabaoth. They come up from the depths of Hell! Will you be able to bear, will you be able to

156

stand up, even in prayer, under that kind of burden, hearing those cries, seeing those torments and the smoke that comes up from that place and the smell of burning flesh? Will you be able to stand it? Will you be able to bear it? Will you care? Will you care? Can I give the burden to you? Will you be faithful? Will you really pray? That is why I cannot give you these things, because if you would leave them, and if you would leave that place and go on your way and take a ho-hum attitude, it would break My heart. For it is life and death we are talking about! It is eternity. It is eternity — a never-ending eternity that we are talking about.

And I am looking for those who are willing to be totally abandoned to Me. I am looking for those who are willing to be shut in like John the Baptist. I am looking for those who are willing to speak forth with boldness the words that I will put in their mouths, without fear or favor. I am not looking for those who will have a message that tickles the ears of the people, for they have been tickled enough! I am looking for those who are willing to speak the truth, the whole truth, of My counsel. I am looking for those who are willing to come to Me for counsel and My counsel alone. I am looking for those who are willing to stand in My counsel and not sit in the seat of the scornful or walk in the way of the ungodly.

It is a narrow path, My children. It's a narrow path and straight is the gate. But look at the teeming millions on the wide road. Look at them. Look at them. They are going on the way to Hell, and who really cares? Who really cares? Who is willing, who's willing to give up even an hour of their time? You're stingy, My children. You are stingy and selfish, for you are not willing. You are thinking only of yourself!

And, oh, I am so sad. It grieves My heart to have to speak harshly to you this morning, but it is the thing that you were wanting to know and that you have been asking Me, and I speak it to you this morning. But I also ask, "Are you willing? Are you willing to go all the way?" Or are you willing to go like the three disciples whom Jesus had to leave because they could not bear it? They could not bear the agony and the tears and the sorrow and the grief and the birthing of what I had to birth.

Are you willing? Will you be willing to do that? Are you willing to be separated unto Me and Me alone? Are you willing?

How to Get a Burden from the Lord

There is no way to desire the souls of men except as you are consumed with a love for Me. It is My love alone, overtaking and overcoming you, that does and will lead you to lay yourself down, to die to self, for the souls of men. Learn of Me, and let Me fill you and tell you of My deep desire for the souls of men. Nothing else matters to Me! That's where My heart is. That's why I weep and My Father weeps and the Holy Spirit weeps and laments over the multitudes going to destruction. And We weep over the saints who refuse to lay aside everything, that they might prepare the way for the salvation of souls.

I desire to save them, just as I did when I went to the Cross. Will you make the way and intercede so I can reach them? Will you make a way in the wilderness of their lives — in the prisons they live in, in the snares in which the devil has them entrapped — that they might be set free and saved? Together there are multitudes we can harvest before night comes and no man can work.

Today — as we commune together, as we pray together — ask Me for that deep, abiding desire for the souls of men. Ask Me to place them upon your heart that I might breathe My life into them. Cry out and take hold of the altar horns and importune for them. Press in and get My heartbroken desire for their souls. To Me they are like jewels, even as you are My jewels, My treasures. Carry them on your heart as I do on Mine, and bring them on the wings of fervent prayer into the presence of your God. Then, wherever I lead, you will follow and labor with My love and the power of the Spirit to bring them forth out of death into My Life.

Call and cry unto Me, and I will show you great and mighty things which you know not, even by My Spirit: how I will bring them forth as you PRAY, PRAY, PRAY as desperate ones — desperate for their Salvation and for My glorification. Not by power nor might, but by My Spirit.

My Love Slaves

Oh My children, that I might find you desiring and willing to share My burdens, to know the lament of My heart. Those who love Me deeply, who desire to be wed to Me at the Marriage Supper — surely they will want to share My deep longings and pain. For I see the multitudes I died for going to eternal damnation because I cannot find many who will be My "love slaves" — not servants, not joint heirs, not adopted sons and daughters, but love slaves. I have great need of you to be My love slaves: those who hear Me call you out to lay down your lives as unto Me for the souls of men. Without you taking commands from Me, even moment by moment, the loss of souls to Hell will only increase!

Do you really love Me? Do you really want to know the deep desires on My heart? Do you really want to labor without reservation for My Kingdom to be established on Earth? Then lay aside every thought and plan and desire of your own, and let Me tell you My ultimate desires: and they are that you fellowship with Me and love Me so zealously that all your desires are to delight My heart and to be obedient to My call.

My heart breaks over the multitudes dying without coming

to Salvation. But you are My chosen generation, My royal priesthood, My holy nation, to show forth My glory by saving souls. Will you not give up everything, that I might possess you as love slaves to do My bidding in this sin-sick world? Oh the joy in Heaven over each lost soul saved. Oh the joy in My heart over each of My children who repents with broken heart over their own sins and toils with broken heart to save sinners. That is your meat, as it was Mine; and you will be strengthened as you set captives free.

Let the power flow from My throne into you and from you, by My Spirit, and see the wondrous things we can accomplish. My Blood has all power to break chains of bondage. In My Name there is all authority over the works of the devil. Then I can deliver.

My love slaves have such commitment, abandonment, love-fervor for Me. They know I can and will do far above that which they ask or think, by the power of the Spirit working in them — even in weeping, groaning, and travailing. Repentance is a way of life with them as they always recognize that they must have more and more of that self-life (which is still in them) removed and crucified. For it will be by My total control in them that My glory is manifested — as all carnality is removed, even burned out.

So, will you be My love slaves? So it was for Paul, James, Jude, and many others; so it was for Me with My Father. Will you say "yes"?

As you respond to My love and let Me court you, we will become better acquainted. I will share with you My heart. I will need you to listen and be genuinely concerned about the needs, griefs, and burdens on My heart as I share them with you. I will need you to pray about them. It is only as you respond to My love and grow to love Me more, that you will be really concerned and touched and moved to the point of intercession with genuineness. I have prepared you for this. Listen, I am teaching you about love.

Calvary Love

When you know how to truly die to yourself, you will be able to intercede with genuine, heart-felt love — Calvary Love — for others. It is My will and My way. Your willingness to die to yourself will bring life to those you make intercession for. You must love freely and be obedient in all that I speak to you about; otherwise you will be too selfish and self-contained to accept another's need as your own. Somewhere in the birthing process you will seek your own desires and abort the baby to save yourself. Your will, your way, your desires and lusts will surface, and you will save yourself. Offenses will come, and you will save yourself.

Heed My call and come. Follow Me all the way to Calvary.

Brokenness

My children, I am looking for those who will not only do My will, but who delight to do My will in glad obedience to Me, moment by moment. That delight comes only from a broken spirit, which comes from the Spirit of the Lamb slain from the foundation of the world. When you deeply desire that slain spirit, that broken spirit, you will gladly yield to Me, and you will desire for Me to shine My searchlight upon your heart and thoughts, to reveal every sin separating you from Me. For there will come upon you a deep desire to totally do My will, My perfect will; for this is the heartfelt desire of My bride.

Come to Me, abandon yourself to Me and for Me and for My use. Sit at My feet and learn of Me, and be taught by Me the way of being broken in your heart, where your spirit is. As you spend more and more time with Me, loving Me more and more and letting Me work in you this new spirit, you will be united with Me. Your heart can even melt and be one with Mine, and *My* heart cry for revival will be *your* heart cry too. And that longing will lead you to join with a holy remnant I am calling and raising up, that will cry out and travail night and day until I rain down revival, upon My people first and then upon the lost.

Do you not see that only as you are wholly Mine in brokenness will you persevere unto revival? Like David you must see your great need for a broken spirit and the poured out life. From your brokenness I will make of you a fountain of living water, My Living Water. For as I give you a broken heart, even My broken heart, then I will pour out My Spirit upon you, and you will be that fountain that will overflow with My Living Water, to go out to the souls at the ends of the earth, even to the hidden away and desolate places. And at the same time, I will give you a vision, a greatly expanded vision, of that which I am doing and will do throughout the earth.

Have you forgotten I am the omnipotent, the omniscient, and the omnipresent One, and I am also the Hound of Heaven, desiring that not one be lost? There are many I will save as you pray, as you have My vision, as you pray by My Spirit, by the power of the Holy Spirit. For I will reveal Myself to many to whom no one will go — to those in the vast expanses, the desert places and wilderness, as it were — but I will go by My Spirit. For I will reveal Myself to them as you pray, as you have a new vision (even My vision of the wondrous things I will do by My Spirit), as you pray and pray and cry out to Me to save in these Last Days, when My grace will be multiplied and sent out to the lost, as you are broken, filled, and refilled with My grace to overflowing.

Press in, press on, break through! Take hold of Me and the horns of the altar until I pour out mighty torrents of Living Water to the uttermost parts of the earth. Never forget I am the One who desires that not one be lost, but that all come to repentance, to Salvation. By My Spirit I will not withhold one good thing, even My grace and mercy, from one soul when My people pray the fervent, effectual prayers for My inheritance to be established in the earth.

I will give you My bowels of mercy for the task, and the power, anointing, and inspiration of the Holy Ghost, as you labor for this End-Time harvest. The best is yet to come in the midst of the great darkness in the earth. For so shall My glory be manifested in one last finale when multitudes greater than you have ever imagined will come forth into the Kingdom of God for all eternity!

So shall it be through a holy remnant, a people ablaze with love for Me and with My passion for souls in these Last Days, a remnant broken and empowered by My Spirit, My divine life flowing in them, saith the Lord.

You Are Under My Divine Appointment

My son, for years your life has been ordered and directed by others. You have spent many hours working for people, working for companies. You have been an obedient employee. You have come and gone as they have instructed you. You have appeared at the time they have told you to. You have taken upon yourself many jobs and tasks that often you thought you could not do, but you have accomplished them. And you have done that for many years, My son. You have been under their rule, as it were, and their appointment, and their timing.

But now, My son, I tell you that you are under My appointment, My divine appointment. For at this time, I, your

163

Heavenly Father, am watching and monitoring and regulating those things that are happening throughout your day now. And I, your Heavenly Father, have your time card, as it were; and I am calling you at different times to come and be in My presence and do My bidding and do My work and My service. And at times it may not seem to you that it is of much consequence — that what you are doing is amounting to very much — because you are not seeing what you think you should see. When you worked with your hands, there were things that you accomplished, and at the end of the day you could see what your hands had done. At the end of the week you were rewarded for your work.

But this, My son, is an eternal appointment, an eternal position, an eternal job that you are doing for Me. It is unto Me and for Me alone. I have prepared you, and I am preparing you, for this job. The hours are not the same, for I will call you at different times. Sometimes it may not be convenient for you. Sometimes you may not feel like responding. This job position can only be afforded by and awarded to those who have given themselves to Me and are willing to come into that secret closet of intimacy and to know Me in that way. For the sharing and the appointing of these job positions and the giving of this that I would have you do, has everything to do with intimacy. It is the sharing of My very heart and burdens.

Even yet there are yearnings in your heart that are keeping you from fully receiving that which I would want you to have and to birth for Me and for the Kingdom. Even now there are grievances in your heart from the past, which you must lay at My feet and know that I will heal you of them — if you will allow Me to, if you will allow Me to shine the light of My Word on your heart, and if you will be willing to face them and know that I can heal you. And it is only I Who can heal you, as you respond to My love, My deep, deep love for you, My son.

You have been called and chosen from your Mother's womb. Do not think that things were a mistake or happened by chance. For you are Mine, My son, called for a specific time and a specific job. You must lay all else aside. You have been sensing this in your heart, but fear is keeping you bound. Fear is keeping you bound. But you must know, My son, at first it will not be as you have supposed. Do not grieve. Do not grieve. Do as I instruct you in the days to come. It is not for this earth; it will not show upon this earth. You will not be paid in earthly money, as it were. But I, I your Heavenly Father, will see to it that you will not lack in any area. So do not be afraid. Do not be afraid, for I will pour out upon you that which you will not have room enough to receive.

So come to Me, My son. Continue to come as you have. For you are more special to Me than I can relate in words, earthly words, that you can understand at this time. But know that I have great need of you — great need of you. Even though you do not stand in places where other people are — people whom you think will receive great recognition — know that you stand before Me, My son. You stand before Me, and I appoint your tasks. Do not be afraid. Come, come to that place of intimacy. Come, look into My eyes, My son, look into My eyes. There I will share with you the needs and the burdens. I will share My love with you in a way that you have not known before, for I love you deeply — deeply.

Do not be afraid. Do not be discouraged. Do not be downhearted. Do not be dismayed. Do not be despondent, My son, do not be. Look up! Look up into the eyes of your Saviour, who loves you and who has called you apart — called you to Himself and called you to His side. You, you, you, My son, I have called you! Do not doubt and do not fear.

The Prayers of My Intercessors

This is the hour I take you off the shelf. I bring you into My sanctuary to pray with Me. This is the day and the hour that I have trained you for. I have brought you through, and you are overcomers. My intercessors are overcomers.

Oh, I flow My Spirit through My intercessors. As they flow unto Me, I flow unto them. As they open their hearts to Me, I open My heart to them. As they pray unto Me, I give them words to pray. I give them the key that will bring down revival.

I give you My heart; I give you My Word. Ferret out My Rhema. Ferret out from My written Word and from My spoken word. Ferret out My promises, My truth for this End-Time.

Pray, pray with authority! Pray, for I have given My children authority. I have given you intercessors authority with which to pray. You have My Name and you have My Blood and you have My Spirit and you have My Word. You shall shake the heavens, and you shall shake the earth. The whole universe shall be shaken by the prayers of My intercessors. And things will happen: things in the heavens, things in the earth, things in the hearts of men. Oh, mighty things are going to happen because of the prayers of My intercessors.*

Oh, I give you a sense of the might and the power of My Army. My Army under My command is an army such as this earth has never seen. People may not see it, but they shall feel the effect of My intercessors, My people of the Spirit, My people who live in the Spirit with Me.*

Oh, I invite you, I command you, to rise up, rise up higher in the Spirit. Yes, yes, let go of the things that cling, those things you don't need. Look up to Me, and I will teach you; I will teach you where your real need is. And I will provide the things of the earth, but look unto Me for the things of Heaven, for the things of the Spirit.

Yes, you are My vessels, you are My clay vessels. But oh, My broken vessels, My vessels of honor you are becoming. You will carry the water of the Spirit. Only broken vessels can carry the water of the Spirit. Only through them can the Spirit flow from under the throne of Heaven. . . .

*This section, and the rest of the prophecy, will come to pass only as God's people are faithful in answering the call to prayer and deeper intercession.

My Control Tower

I am calling you, My child, to fast and pray for My Church. You want to be free of jealousy and envy and indifference and apathy concerning your brothers and sisters in the Church. This is the way, through fasting and prayer, to come into My love for My Church. As you fast, and as you pray with Me, I will share with you My suffering and lamenting and My prayer and intercession for them.

I am asking you to come into My Control Tower, the Holy of Holies, with Me. You will watch, and learn and share My burdens. You will be safe and secure with no fear, for I love you; and I desire your fellowship and friendship, your CONSTANT companionship. You are important to Me. I call you to come away with Me to My Control Tower — the hub of Earth's affairs, of Earth's people, and beyond! Here I will share secrets with you and your prayer partner. Both of you are coming away with Me to My Control Tower.

I work differently and uniquely with each of My children, but My end goal — a fruitful life bringing glory to My Father, assisting Me as I bring many sons into His Kingdom; and a life of holiness and worship, dwelling and abiding in My presence — is the same for each of My children.

As you have known in your spirit and yearned for in your spirit, you shall come deeper and deeper into My heart. You shall always have My presence. You are never alone. When fear of loneliness attacks you, always choose joy. Joy in Me — in My presence, in our sharing many adventures together — and joy in My constant love for you, which seems to grow as you become more and more aware of it. You will become acutely sensitive in your spirit (just as you have become acutely sensitive to the least ache or pin-prick pain or feeling that something is wrong in your body). You desire and I desire you to have that acute spiritual sensitivity.

As I clear your calendar, you will spend more and more time in the Holy of Holies being a priestly intercessor for My Church. You already know you need not try in the flesh to give equal time or an equal number of prayers for the lost and the Church. I am the conductor of the orchestra of sweet smelling and sweet sounding prayers rising to Me from My praying remnant. You just pray as I, My Holy Spirit, inspires you to pray.

Exciting times are ahead for My intercessors — exciting adventures in the Spirit realm. Go with the flow of My Spirit, the anointing of My oil upon your heads, running down over you. You will dance and sing with Me, but most important now, we will work together in these last seconds of time on Earth (and in My universe) to bring ALL My sheep into My Father's family, into His Kingdom and into My bride.

Yes, these things are extremely important to Me, but it is My desire that you not be overwhelmed anymore to the point of fear of trying. I am God, the Lord: King of all kings and nations and governments. I hold time in My hands, and the life of each leader and of each follower in My hands. I know your heart-cries and heart-needs and your physical needs as a human being, for I lowered Myself to be Emmanuel in an earthly body. I will take care of your health and your food, clothing, shelter, and car needs; for you are My beloved child and bride-to-be, now My betrothed by the seal of My Holy Spirit.

Trust and obey is truly all you need do. Do not worry, fret, look back at the past, nor think Satan's thoughts of confusion and negativeness. Think on Me, and Me only, and upon the true emphasis of My Word that I am teaching you now by My Holy Spirit. Put your mind upon Me in all ways and upon My suffering, and the flesh that clings to you will melt as wax before the fire. Keep your eyes upon Me as I burn off the flesh, and you will feel no true pain. You will be surprised and, oh, so joyful one day when you notice how much flesh I have burned off!

By My Spirit power freely flowing into you and through you constantly, My bondservant, you can do ALL that I ask you to do!

The Life of the Intercessor

I will not hold the life of intercession before you without enabling you to live it. I am asking for a closer, more obedient walk from you. I am working in you to cause you to seriously believe that you can walk this life. I come to you in many ways. You are learning to know Me in all My ways. I am here now as your Friend, and we are fellowshipping as I teach you. I am here as your Teacher. You know Me as a mighty Warrior in intercession. But you need more time with Me as your Warrior-King.

In battle, we cannot make mistakes of judgment. In battle, we need instant, correct judgment of the situation. In battle, you need complete trust in your Warrior-King. In battle, we are totally serious, for the future destination of the lost, the backslidden, and My precious Jews is at stake. In battle, self must be dead on the cross you carry to Golgotha. In battle, your will has no life of its own. In battle, your broken heart is strong-hearted because it leans totally on Me. In battle, your heart and the eyes of your spirit hear and see and obey My slightest, quietest word to you. You see with My eyes, you understand with My heart. In battle, you are strong-hearted and steadfast and unquestioning, and you never give up, because ever in your heart and ever in your tears are those we battle for.

As a true soldier your thoughts are ever on the next battle, the battle to come, and on the reason you are a soldier — and that is to intercede for the lost of every nation, tribe, and tongue; the children killed before birth, abused after birth, and taught there is no God of righteousness, truth, mercy, and love for them; the old, sick, and abused; the poor, the unloved, the prisoner of self and flesh and the devil; the mentally ill; and on and on.

As a soldier your communication is terse and to the point, your mind clear and not entangled with personal and family problems. You have only one driving force in body, mind, and spirit and that is to persevere in doing your job correctly in the position I have given you in My Army.

Everything you do (wherever you are), everything you think in your mind, everything you say to any person and to Me, must be subject to and pertain to My Spirit, and flow by My Spirit through you, to build you up in Me (inner eyes on Me alone) in the position I have called you to in My End-Time Army of Intercessors. You are in battle, and you have no time off. You are either on alert or fighting, interceding day and night!

No idle words can pass your lips, else we lose a battle! No idle, light-hearted thoughts or memories can occupy your mind, lest you do not see the attack of the enemy, and one you are here to protect, call out, and raise up in Me will perish by a silent blow of the enemy. One at a time the lost are saved, but also one at a time they go over the edge of Hell and are lost forever!

I am calling you to a seriousness of life deeper in Me than I have ever called you to before. Your words, thoughts, and actions affect someone's eternity. Without Me, that is too heavy a burden for you; without Me, that will crush you in body, mind, and spirit. But I walk beside you; you are yoked with Me; and this burden is light if you stay yoked in harness with Me. Only with Me can you go through this fire. Only with Me can you go through these waters. Only with Me will you survive the End-Time battles.

Yes, I am the Leader, Teacher, Trainer, Exhorter, and Commander of My Army. There is great spiritual fellowship as you camp with, train with, and fight with your fellow soldiers. Great love develops in you to the laying down of your life for a fellow soldier — as well as for a lost one, and as well as for Me — at My command, only without question!

I have and will continue to equip you and train you with all My weapons of attack and a few of defense. But we in these End-Times are an army of attack. Like Gideon, under your Warrior-King's anointing, you will have no fear and no doubts. Even you have I given a warrior's heart — a strong, persevering, thoroughly broken, crushed heart — at your request. Even you can and will submit your will to Mine, in an instant! Choose this day whose army you will serve in. This day we will begin your induction and training.

Love, faith, obedience, surrender, repentance, brokenness are the watch-words of My Army. Remember them well. We will come together in a victory banquet the likes of which the earth has never seen!

Pray in tongues at all times!

The Fervency of My Heart

Oh, do not get caught up in anything of the world. Seek Me moment by moment every day. Look up, look up in anticipation of Me; and pray with all the fervency that's on My heart — not your heart, but MY heart. I want to give you the fervency of MY heart. That is My desire. And as you fellowship with Me and as you love Me — love Me — and let Me continually bring you to repentance and cleanse you, it will be the fervency of MY heart that I will impart to you. And with that fervency will come the power from On High. For I never give a desire for fervency without providing the power — if My children will so desire to be what I have called them to be, and totally surrender to Me.

But I say, do not get caught up in even the slightest things of the world, but keep walking through the world on that "highway to Heaven," yearning for Me and wanting to be My love slaves — with your eyes fixed on Me, your hearts knit together with Me. For just as I was always that Love Slave to My Father, so you too, then, will be love slaves unto Me and servants unto men. Not the other way around. And your only desire will be to glorify Me and fulfill My desires — as you love Me with all your heart, soul, mind, and strength.

And your eyes will be fixed on Me. And those who have that dove vision and those who will be purified, they shall see Me. And when you see Me, nothing else will matter to you.

Always remember that if you're going to wait to be prepared tomorrow, it may be too late. For I am coming very soon, very soon! And this is the day of preparation, and this is the day of harvesting, and this is the day to be full of the oil from the Spirit — and tomorrow and the next day and the next, humbly seeking Me and loving Me, that I might give you My fervent, broken heart. That's where the power is, My children; that *is* the power. And that power from the fervent, broken heart is that which distills and brings down the rain from Heaven for revival.

Test All Things

Give up friends and phone calls that break the anointing of My Spirit — even family. Only be about My work for you — intercession! No fruitless meetings or journeys. Test them! Test all by My fruits. Do they produce My harvest fruit? If not, the answer is "no!" Do they line up with your work in My Kingdom? If not, the answer is "no!"

You have prayed for My power to answer your prayers. That same power will work in you to bring you to obedience — even quickly! By My Spirit!

Be Instant in Season

My dear children — obedience! The obedience I am asking and requiring of you, so you can be used effectively and effectually in this day, is not only that of obeying My written Word, though I do want that, but I am looking for you to obey ME, the Living Word, when I call. For I call day and night, whenever there is a need. You must be ready, alert to come — to intercede, to battle — at My beckon call. You must live "on alert" all the time, dressed for and ready for battle, as it were. Timing is everything! You must get up and pray THE INSTANT I call. When a soul is drowning, when one is trapped in a burning building, rescue is required IMMEDIATELY! So it is when I call you to that kind of rescuing. It can't wait for a convenient time.

Ask Me to make you "instant in season." Ask Me to give you a sensitivity to My call that you have never had before. Ask to have all resistance, lethargy, and apathy burned out, and ask that you have My passion for rescuing souls as never before. It only comes in those who love Me above all else. It requires the greatest devotion to Me. I have told you I will not withhold any good thing from you if you ask with right and pure motives. Ask, ask, ask!

Only by the power of the Spirit making you an overcomer — overcoming all self-life, making you tried and proven and trained for this kind of sensitive obedience — will you become that one, instant in season, at My beckon call. It's My End-Time call to My bondservant intercessors.

Do you see the necessity? Can you hear the urgency in My voice? Will you obey instantaneously? Bow before Me and ask the Holy Spirit to teach you, to "sensitize" you to this obedience. It is deep calling to deep. Oh, listen, listen for My call. Then hear and obey. It is by the Spirit as our hearts are knit together.

The devil is prowling around seeking whom he might devour, whom he might deceive, whom he might ensnare in many insidious ways; and I need My intercessors to be ready to step in at My call — IMMEDIATELY. That, My beloved, is the kind of obedience I am looking for. Fine-tuned ears come from hearts fine-tuned to Me, to My voice, night and day. They are My holy ones, those wholly Mine, who will crucify the flesh.

Do as I Did

What have you done for Me, My child? What has your hand produced? What have you done by the sweat of your brow? What has your heart wrought? Where is the fruit of your lips? Nothing, nothing can *you* do. Only by My Spirit can the fruit of your lips become sweet praise, thundering warnings, and fervent prayers!

You must learn to yield to Me, to My Holy Spirit, My child, as a bride yields to her bridegroom. Cease from your striving, from your works, My child. Come into the quiet. Wait upon Me. Allow Me to woo you. Be still and know that I am gentle and patient in My love for you. Let Me quiet your spirit as I minister to you, as I serve you. No, I shall never tire of serving My lovely bride.

My child, together with Me, we are one. But to really know Me, to serve Me, to love Me, you must always be watching Me — watching My every word and My every move. Do as I did with My Father. I did everything He spoke, and in that way I served Him and serve you and so many, many others. Watch Me in My Word! Hear by the Spirit what I speak to you each day: It may be in My Word, or it may be in a word like this, or it may be from the heart of a servant like you.

Think on the things I did each day. First, in the morning I went away by Myself, into a garden or up a hill. It is not wrong to go away by yourself, if you then pray. And then I served My Father by teaching and healing, doing miracles and all the works of the Holy Spirit. Why could I do these things? I was filled with the power of the Holy Spirit and motivated with the Father's love, for you and for many multitudes, then and now.

Come to Me. And as I fill you with My love, your love shall come up higher into My love and will be transformed into Holy Spirit power that will energize and motivate you to powerful, fervent prayer for all peoples and all nations. And you will have My strength to bear the daily, hourly burden of very, very lost souls.

You are afraid to come with Me and watch with Me and weep with Me over this very heavy burden for the lost. You are afraid of spiritual warfare with Me, fearing I will leave you and even fearing that I will not come and be with you through each battle — before we begin until after we end. My child, you are learning to trust in Me for prayer and victory. Trust in Me also that when you still your soul and stir up your heart, I will immediately come to you so we can intercede together till our prayers break through and are answered. I will never fail to come to you in our chamber of prayer. You will not need to wait for hours. I will come after you have prepared yourself for battle with conviction of and repentance from sin, and after you have sent the devil away in My Name and with My Blood.

Peace, peace, My child, and meet Me again in a few hours!

The Breaker

My son, did I not say to you that I am the Breaker? I am the One that goes before and clears the way, and I would have you to know, My son, that you are My apprentice; you are the one that is also breaking and going before. You are tearing down many walls, many hindrances, in prayer. And even as you have put in physical labor in these past weeks and you have lifted many things and moved many things, so you have done the same in the Spirit, My son; you have done the same. And it has been exhausting, and there is even more work to do, for many of the walls, many of the barriers, are very thick and very heavy; but I know that you will persevere and that you will not give up, you will not give up for tiredness. I know that. I know your heart; I know that I can trust you.

And so I say, My son, do not be weary, for *you* are also a breaker. You are going forth, you are breaking through, you are preparing the way. And so, My son, do not be discouraged and do not grow weary in well doing, for you shall see an end, you shall reap as you faint not. And know that in the days ahead there is much to be done, much to be done in the Spirit, and I need you. I need your hands, as it were, in the Spirit. I need you to come and to lift and to pull and to push and to bring forth and to make a way and to clear the way — to clear the way for the coming of the Lord and the work that I am about to do.

So do not be discouraged, for I am the Lord your God and I am helping you. It is My strong right arm, it is My hands that are holding you, that are helping you. But My heart is so touched because you are willing, you are a willing worker; and even though you have been weary, weary even unto death sometimes, you have not given up; and that is more than I have asked, and I am pleased. And I will help you and enable you to do an even greater work in the days ahead. So do not be weary, My son, for you walk alongside of Me, you work alongside of Me, the Breaker, and the way shall be clear.

Pray My Word

I am your Warrior-King! When you have battles to fight, call upon Me to fight for My Word. I fight on behalf of My Word, for My Word shall be accomplished. Use My Word as your flashing sword. Use it in battle. Do not be afraid. Do not hang back. Have I not given you full authority to call upon My Name and to plead your case before Me? Use My Word to plead your case. Look, look, look into the Book. I will reveal its meaning. I will teach you the Word to use in intercession on behalf of the peoples, tongues, tribes in the deserts, and nations you pray for. I have a Word for every nation, for every conflict between nations, for every situation among nations and in national and world governments, just as I do in people's lives.

Yes, you have spent much time learning how My Word applies to the individual lives of My people. Now is the time for you to come a step higher and apply My Word, the Word of the prophets, to My world.

Come, be not afraid, for I will teach you a new thing. There is battle among nations, spiritual battles, going on at all times. I want you, My children, to fight in these battles. Do not fret over what you do not know in your mind, for My strategies are far above your mind anyway. I have strategies I will use to get nations to do My bidding. I have more strategies to bring more lost into My Eternal Kingdom than you (or even the devil) can ever imagine. With My Army doing My commands, we will keep the enemy so confused, he will not grasp My strategies, and, just as when My Son became man, I will cause My strategies to come to pass right under his nose. But he will not smell the truth until the battle and the war are long finished!

My desire is to give you insight and understanding of My battle plan for the particular battles I put upon your hearts. (You that pray together — I give you the same battles to fight.) I want you to stretch out into My Spirit and see and know My strategies, My thoughts, and My creative battle plans, taken right from My prophetic Word, and supported and confirmed by My Spirit throughout My Book of My Word.

Be not afraid. Step out into the little known and the little understood. Do not worry whether or not it is according to My Word as you step out — you will soon see if you sink or if you are upheld in your use of My flashing Sword! Be not afraid of mistakes. They will not cause Me to move contrary to My Word [when you are in error]. Be sensitive in the Spirit — alert, watchful of Me and My flashing Sword at ALL times. You will learn under My teaching and guidance.

But unless you trod previously untrod ground, you will only be an observer. My Army is for doers of My Word. Put your faith into action. Be motivated by My agape love for every single lost soul and every people-group of lost souls. Yours are the hidden duties, hidden from the eyes of man, but they are the very foundation of My many victories even now being won in the hearts and changed lives of men, women, and children, who now have hope for eternal life, throughout every nation, every soil trod by the foot of man.

Speak, speak out My Word for the world's people, as you speak it for yourself and your families and friends. Pray your heart prayer and heart desires now for My dying world — then there need be no question in your hearts that I will preserve, protect, lead, and teach your own children, as you do this new thing in your hearts and lives.*

I need you, an intercessor and doer of My Word as I have spoken it in ages past, to accomplish My will for these exciting End-Times. I invite you, I command My bondservants, to take part in My End-Time battles. Oh My children, look and see once again the end results: the many multitudes of souls who will march upright and free into My Heavenly Kingdom because you pray My plan for the world and its people and its nations and governments. And then watch once again the conveyor belt of souls being carried away to the edge of Hell, where they are soon to be dumped over the edge to begin their descent into the abyss of eternal separation from Me.

Where would you rather be? By My Spirit and My mighty right arm bared for battle, you can give them the truth with which to make a fully informed decision for their eternity. With your intercession, My people and My Chosen People will not perish after all. Be creative with My Word. Look and listen and pray My Word, so that it may accomplish the great and final task I sent it out to accomplish.

I am your victorious Warrior-King! Follow Me into the final war, into the final hour.

*That is, as you pray for the world's people and for God's dying world.

179

A Warring Spirit

[Our cry to God]: "Until You come and purify us, until You come and break us, so we can become that priesthood that You have called us to be, we won't let go!"

[God's reply]: I desire that you "wrestle" with Me [see Isaiah 64:7a]; I desire that.* That is the humility and that is the kind of commitment and courage I am looking for in My people — that they will come, and they will cry out and persevere before Me and say: "Lord, we will not let go until You break us, until You break us and show us every sin that separates us from You, until You send the wind, even Your power, and until You send the fire, even Your purifying fire, that we can be pure and holy, wholly Yours, Lord."

I desire that you ask for that, My children; I desire that in My people. For when I have a people who will wrestle with Me — who so desire Me to have My way in them — I will give them courage and boldness, I will give them humility and meekness. This is that warring spirit, the spirit that is in vessels which I will fill with My bowels of mercy and with perseverance until victory comes.

Oh My children, that is the spirit I desire to put in you: the importuning, persevering spirit, the spirit of selling out to Me, that I might have My way and that I might give you that power from On High that will bring forth My glory and will accomplish things that are far above all you can ask or think. Don't think your thoughts, but think the way I think. I will not withhold any good thing from you. I will not withhold that cleansing and breaking and purifying you desire — when you cry out for it. And those vessels, those broken vessels with that new spirit, that "other spirit" — that spirit that cries out — will then go forth in My power.

You will see what the enemy is doing, you will see the darkness and the destruction, but you will look up and you will behold My face and My glory, and you will know that that which I can do, that which I will do in the earth, is so much greater than the darkness and destruction. For where My Light and My glory shine forth, multitudes shall come into the Kingdom. And as you pray, as you pray as those tenacious vessels who will not let go of Me until I pour forth My anointing upon you — if you will importune that way, wrestle that way with Me — I will do it; and the great things that shall be accomplished, they shall be according to My plans and purposes in My people.

That is the remnant I am calling forth, cleansed by My purifying fire, who will not stop persevering until My glory is poured out; those are the ones who will see My glory. When they see My glory, they will desire that My glory be poured out upon the earth — and that glory is the Revival Fire! (But the preparation for revival must first come as wind and fire and brokenness in My own people.) And there will be no place too far away, there will be no place too dark or too deep, there will be no life too hopeless to save. No, there is no such thing when I have a people who will persevere that way.

Oh, pray that My intercessors will understand and importune and wrestle with Me and then wrestle for the souls of men. Oh yes, that is My desire, and I shall have such a people. And I desire you to be among that remnant that looks up and is seated in heavenly places, and is going forth with My eyes and My vision and with My glory upon them; and through them it shall be poured out upon men, women, and children in this dark world for a great harvest.

Nothing, nothing is too hard if you will persevere in that brokenness. It is a journey for the rest of your lives. Be broken to delight to do the Father's will, and your heart will not condemn you. You will be free, and you will rejoice in that continual brokenness that allows Me to have My way in you. It will release you. You will be released, and joy will flow and new strength will come. For I will bring forth those rivers of Living Water, and there will be nothing holding them back!

Oh, this is the road I want you to walk on. It is the narrow way; it is the way on which I lead; it is the way of the Cross. For the way of the Cross is that of brokenness, and it leads to glory, both in your lives and in the lives of those around you (those whom you are praying for): for intercessors, for that remnant I am bringing out of the Church, and for the backslidden, the lost, and My beloved People, Israel. It is the only way.

Yes, yes, I love those who will wrestle with Me for that life. And I shall give it to you as long as you stay humble and persevere in deep *and* deeper intimacy with Me. And out of My presence you will come forth with My power. Again I say, there is no other way.

Oh My people, I am the same yesterday, today, and forever. I have not changed. When My people will pray those fervent prayers, when those humble vessels — those who will sit before Me, love and adore Me, with their eyes fixed on Me and their hearts knit together with Mine — will pray those kinds of prayers, then the power of My anointing will break down the strongest strongholds.

So look, look unto Me, and live with Me (seated in heavenly places), journey with Me, think on Me, love Me with a zeal as never before, and see if I will not open those floodgates of Heaven and pour out those blessings I desire to pour out upon My anointed vessels. For I have great and mighty things I want to do through you which you have not yet seen. (You have heard reports of them taking place in My persecuted Church around the world.)

Come to Me in love — in reverential fear and awe — and that fear you have of giving up the "good life," of giving up the things of the earth, will grow dim and go. For My Love will cause you to see that your life of ease is not the life you really desire. That life of ease you have clung to — it is nothing, nothing! I do not want you to live on your beds of ease; I want you to live in My presence, and I want to live in your heart. But until your heart is pure and consumed with a love for Me, and worldliness is gone, you will not be empowered from On High. Those things contaminate and weigh you down, and I will not dwell in unclean vessels.

Come unto Me and let Me fill you with My treasures, even My very Life, even My very Spirit, even the love and the mercy that you yearn for, and you will actually fling away those other things! But you must desire that life and say, "I delight to do Your will, Heavenly Father. Whatever it takes to work that in me, do it, Heavenly Father, through the Holy Spirit. I hate, I don't want the worldly things I've been clinging to."

Put your treasures, My children, in the things of Heaven, where moth and rust doth not corrupt, even in the work we have to do. For it is a hard work, a toil, but it is the work I have prepared you for. And it is the only work that will bring you true joy, for it is the work that will bear fruit for all eternity. This is the life which you desire because it is what I desire for you. It is the life that glorifies the Heavenly Father.

Live in Me and desire to please Me more than anything. For it is that life of the branch on the vine with your Heavenly Father, the Husbandman, that is the joy life. It's the life you've been searching for, and I give it unto you. Only receive and go forth and persevere.

*"wrestle with God:" to persevere in prayer with God, for Him to have His will and His way in our hearts and lives.

The Remnant and Prayer

Things are coming to pass and falling into place. Things that needed to be done for a long time are now happening. Things are being repaired and purchased, moved, cleaned, and cleared. There is a clearness and a clarity that is being uncovered and coming forth. Everything is being put in place.

This order and bringing together and repairing and cleaning and moving is not only touching the things around you, it is becoming very visible also in the bringing together and joining together of people. Many a faithful servant who has sought Me diligently as a single person will be brought together with a person of like kindred spirit. Great will be their joy; it will be beyond their comprehension.

I will bring together people of like precious faith, hearts that seek Me and Me alone. There will be no question in their minds that God has brought them together — seemingly from out of nowhere. It is My working; it is My plan. These are holy unions. The world, and even some friends, may not understand. Know this: that all joining together in the natural has been divinely appointed in the spiritual. I am even now joining people together in prayer groups, little bands here and there. They shall pray as I direct.

This is not a fairy tale. This is the working of your Almighty Father. I have purposed it; I have planned it. I will do all My pleasure.

An Elijah Company

Yes, My child, I would speak to you. You are My sweet daughter. I have you in your place in My Army. Keep seeking My face and My heart in repentance. Humble yourself before Me, and I will lift you up — up into the high places, to the top of Mount Zion and higher. Fly with Me as the eagle

184

flies, straight up to the Son of Righteousness. Oh, I have planned glorious adventures for you and Me together — in the high places, in the low places, at the edge of the holes to Hell! Yes, My child, together we will rescue the perishing!

Come to Me in quietness and in strength, knit together with Me and your sister and brother, too. Together we four will soar to heavenly heights and swoop as the eagle straight to our target, to catch and lift high the perishing ones. Your prayer partners also have a greatly enlarged heart for the perishing. Together you three and I make four, a company in My Army. By My Spirit we are an Elijah company. I have many Elijah companies in My Army.

Today, My daughter, I brought you into a new glory realm of My Spirit. Your prayers are fervent and effective by My Spirit. Continue following in perfect trust where I lead you in prayer. Your work is eternal. Ask, and I will keep you broken, repentant, humble, free from deception, and protected by My Blood from all the wiles of the enemy.

Come, come dance in the Spirit with Me! Dance for joy over the perishing who have been rescued! Come, come, soar up to the Son of Righteousness with Me, and I will reveal My heart to you, one area at a time. Even now in My heart is the truth.

All must be cleansed. Every grain of wheat must be stored. My threshing floor must be swept clean. The grapes of My wrath must be crushed. New wine must be poured into new wineskins. The righteous will be recognized as My wise virgin — ready, alert, listening for My far-off cry of joy, and aware of My eagerness to embrace My bride and lead her to our wedding feast.

Yes, all of My creation — the stars in the black heavens, the rocks on the coastlines, the birds in the air, the sea creatures, the flowers of the field, the reeds in the water; and most of all My people, My precious loving ones, adoring ones, foolish and lavish in their abandonment to Me, in their bridal love for Me — oh, how they shall joy in our wedding dance! Oh, we will dance the dance of love, the dance of mercy and compassion and grace fulfilled! Oh, for you to be complete in Me, My bride. Oh, what raptures of delight await us in our secret garden, My lovely bride. Oh, the day is so near, so near. Your preparation will soon be complete.

My cup of mercy [God's time of grace] upon this earth's people is soon to be full to the brim. Then shall My cup of wrath be poured out upon this earth and its inhabitants. Come, come away with Me, My bride, when you have been tested and tried and found true, not lacking in your preparations for the day of our union as bride and Groom.

Revival or Revolution[27]

"Wilt thou not revive us again, that thy people may rejoice in thee?" (Psalm 85:6)

It is time that you have another revival. There is no joy in the land. Sin has made the nations of the world desolate. The hearts of My people are full of sadness. There is destruction on every side. My children are fighting each other, and they are rebelling against My anointed leadership. Council meeting after council meeting cannot solve the problems, for the demon spirits that divide come to every business meeting. The only kind of meeting they cannot stand is true Holy Ghost anointed travailing intercessory prayer meetings! Every other kind of committee meeting is their opportunity to breed and sow discord and hard feelings, which cause bitterness.

It is almost impossible in these evil days even to talk things over peaceably with your neighbor, your friend, your co-worker, or your family member. And as for your enemy, it is even more difficult. But you can talk to Me, and I can hear and intervene. And the way I will is by changing hearts

186

through revival. That is why My people need revival, and they need it NOW! They need it badly!

If revival does not come soon, there will be disasters in many ministries and in many churches, for there is a terrible wave of discontentment in the hearts of My people. Demons of jealousy, power-play, criticism, gossip, and false, so-called "gifts of discernment" are operating in full force, trying to tear down the walls of Salvation.

Cry out to Me for revival, and travail and fast for revival! Preach for revival; speak it into existence, and live revival in your heart. It will come, it must come. Yea, it must come now!

Rending the Curtain for Revival Rain

You are in My Army, and My soldiers never stop fighting. They wrestle against the enemy for souls day and night, waking and sleeping. Souls to be saved are always their prayer, unceasingly!

There is a curtain — a strong curtain, but not iron — between you and Heaven. This curtain you must break through. This strong veil must be rent. It will take an army of skillful swordsmen to cut through this curtain with their blades of solid steel. They must work — pray in unison — as one mighty warrior. Pray for My intercessors to hear Me, to hear My call and commands of how to pray and what to pray for. Seek not your own mind, your earthly knowledge, but seek My mind as well as My heart. Then you will know My ways by which I accomplish My acts. Seek the way through the veil for your prayers, and I will reveal it to you. Seek, and I will make sure you find. My seekers must be constant and persistent, like the friend knocking at midnight.

The devil's army is poised like a flood, just as My revival

rain is poised like a flood. Which shall it be, now? Which shall fall upon this earth's people next, now? The choice is My intercessors.' Yes, you can move My hand. You can influence My choice. You can rend the curtain and let revival rain trickle down and then flood onto the earth. Or you can sit at ease. Always you have the choice. Daily and hourly, you make the choice. Which shall it be for you? How much of My love do you have in your heart? Enough to give up ALL, all that worldly life calls you to? Will you see with the eyes of your spirit into the world of My Spirit?

Do you see the horde of the enemy? Do you see the chains and the slippery slide to Hell? Is your heart moved? And do you see My angel army awaiting that tear in the curtain so they can hold back the horde while My intercessors send up prayers, and I answer those prayers through the holes in the curtain?

If you choose to pay the cost, those holes will grow bigger until the curtain is gone, and then My revival rain will fall, and flood all flesh! — men, women, even children and babies, as you have so longed to see. Choose! Choose! Be My bondservant, or a slave to Satan! Choose: multitudes for My Kingdom — Heaven — or multitudes for Hell!

Much More

Much more, much more! There is much more I want to share with you, much more I need you to intercede for. Continue to come, and be faithful, My beloved. I see your willingness to pray for those I've instructed you to pray for — doing it for Me — with no thought of gain, and expecting nothing in return. I will continue to direct and show and tell you what and how to pray. I will pray for you. Continue to make yourself available. Seek Me, love Me with all your heart, O faithful servant of the Lord.

6. Israel

The Bride in Action (II)

Israel, God's Beloved Pastureland[28]

"For He is our God; and we are the people of His pasture, and the sheep of His hand. . . ." (Psalm 95:7)

Yes, I am your Shepherd, and you, My people, are the sheep of My pasture. I hold you in the palms of My hands. The Scripture was My Word to Israel. Israel was My pasture. I loved and still love the land of Israel. The whole of the land is My pastureland for My people, Israel.

As a shepherd farmer loves and knows every square inch of his land — every hill, every valley, every spring, every stream, every cave — so I know Israel. My eyes watch over it from the beginning of the year to the end of it. [see Deuteronomy 11:12] I see everything that happens to it — every building built, every tree planted, every crop raised. I see it all.

I see My people who live in this, My pastureland. I am the Good Shepherd, and My people, Israel, are the sheep of My pasture. I hold My sheep in My hand. I give them personal, intimate handling. If they are in trouble or need Me, all they need to do is call upon Me and I will answer. [see Jeremiah 33:3a] I will deliver them.

I am not only protecting Israel (My pasture) for Israel's, My people's sake; I am doing it for My sake, for I love it. It is the land of My birth. I will not give it to strangers in

189

these Last Days. I will soon move into Jerusalem. Next time, Jerusalem, not Nazareth or Capernaum, will be the place of My residence. There it is that My "congress" will be in session. The law shall go out from Jerusalem. [see Isaiah 2:3c]

Because you have been grafted into spiritual Israel, rejoice, for all these promises are yours also.

The Growth of Anti-Semitism[29]

I have heard your cries, and I have seen your tears for My people in exile. I have seen their tears also; and I have wiped them from the eyes of many who have come home. But there are still multitudes who are weeping to return to the Land that I gave their forefathers. I say unto thee, their weeping shall not be in vain, for I made your tears to be mingled with their tears to make an "ocean" for them to sail on. I need your faith to prepare a ship for them so that they can board a "faith-ship" and sail to the Land of Promise.

Know the Vision

I say unto thee: You sit here and wait for My return; but it is true what the prophets have said: that before I can return and appear to My people, I must gather them from all nations, and then shall the end be. Again I say unto thee, I want you who know the vision, to become involved more than you [have been]. You are involved with your own personal problems, but I want you to become involved with the situation that concerns the eschatology of these days — the winding up of all the affairs and the fulfilling of prophecy, even the days that the prophets desired to look into.

Yea, My children, you are now living in that day of fulfillment. I say unto thee, the things thou hast heard and that thou hast been taught, are now beginning to come to pass all around you. Yea, lift up your eyes and behold and see that this is the End Time. . . . Time has come almost to a total stop for you.

Terrible Persecution of the Jews to Follow

But before the clock stands still for you and these days of grace shall be finished forever, I say unto thee, while there is yet a second of grace, that it is within these days of grace and these hours of grace and while the world is under the promise of grace, that they must come out. For once the grace on the land where they have lived is lifted, there will be no more moving about. I say unto thee, once the Church is taken out, terrible persecution will come upon every Jew in every nation, including the shores of America, Canada, Australia, and the Western lands that seem to be more liberal and kind.

Therefore, you must work hard to save them now out of the lands whither they have wandered. For only as the Jews stand together in the days of the Tribulation, will they have any safety after the Rapture takes place. For even as it was in the days of Esther — that when the decree went out against them, the Jews banded together — so they must now come to their land to band together, or they will be wiped out in the nations.

This is an emergency in this hour such as you can hardly grasp. Don't only wait for My return; I say unto thee, get under the burden for them to return. *For they must return! The heavens await the return of the Jews to the land of Israel!* Therefore, you must become involved in their return, and you must pray more than you do, and you must speak more than you do about it. You must also sacrifice and help them to get to Israel more than you are doing now!

Yea, I say unto thee, many will not hear what the Spirit is saying, for even many of the churches are becoming deaf. There is a spirit of darkness falling over the eyes, even of My Church, and many of them are already turning to persecute the Jews and Israel in their hearts and from their pulpits. I say unto thee, this is the darkness of the Tribulation hour, and many of the churches that teach and preach against the Jews shall themselves suffer in the Tribulation. They shall know of the sword and the blood!

Oh My children, keep your message pure, keep it clean. Sound out the warning! The hour is very late, and they must come from afar. They must return! Yea, I say unto thee, they will not all have returned, they will not all have returned to their land before the last grains of sand have fallen through the hourglass, and the angel, with the message of the End-Time, flies across the skies of the world and cries, "Time shall be no more!" For even now, this angel — who holds the hourglass of the End-Time — even now this angel stands on the threshold of glory waiting for the Lord, the Father, the Maker of Heaven and Earth, to commission it to fly. And yea, I only wait that more will get home, that more will return to Israel.

Satan Seeks to Hinder in Every Possible Way

Satan has used every method within his means — even the religious Jews, to prevent their own people from coming home. Did they not cause the judgment to fall upon Jerusalem the first time? Are they not of the same spirit as those of old who caused that the city should be ransacked and the Temple should be destroyed? Yea, and I say unto you, that spirit is still in Jerusalem.

Yea, and it is in the heart of every self-righteous one who tries to force his thoughts and viewpoints upon those who walk by faith and love. I say unto thee, pray for them, for they are blind with the same blindness that filled and possessed the heart of Saul of Tarsus.

But I say unto thee that I am able to meet them; but I want you to pray, for your prayers can push back the powers of religious darkness and prejudice and fears and suspicions and hatred and unforgiveness. Yea, your prayers can push them back and make a way for Me to come down, even as I came down on the road to Damascus and stopped Saul on his pathway of persecution and vengefulness. I will meet these Jews too, but I need your prayers and compassion for them.

Therefore, cry out for the Orthodox Jew! Cry out for the Hassidic Jew! Cry for the man who walks in darkness! Do not do it in anger, but do it in sisterly and brotherly love, for know that if you had sat in their place, you would feel what they feel.

A Warning to the Church About Its Anti-Semitic Spirit[30]

I would have My people seek deliverance from their inborn spirit of anti-Semitism, inherited from their fathers to the third and fourth generation and beyond, even from the beginning of the enmity of Satan against My Chosen People.

Boast not yourselves against the original branches, because it is only by the grace given in their roots that you are able to stand before Me, saith the Lord who will yet vindicate Israel. And where will you stand in that day when I finally exalt and restore them? — you who have succumbed to apathy and trepidation, to dissuade yourselves and distract yourselves from imparting My Spirit of new Life to My old branches.

You support them with your mouth in token ways, but I see the deep, dark, hidden recesses of your hearts — and I tell you that they are not yet perfect toward My People, the Jews.

Your lip service will not suffice; but in this time I will even require that you lay down your lives for your brother, the olive tree of Israel, the planting of the Lord which shall never be uprooted.

Cleanse yourselves of your secret sin — a residue of anti-

Semitic indoctrination from all your childhood. I will discern and I will mightily bless those who put My first-born people first, who assist Me in My first priority at this climax of history and prophecy. You will receive your reward double, for the mouth of the Lord has spoken it.

Cease Not to Pray for Jerusalem

Oh, how many times I would have drawn you unto Myself, and you would not. O Jerusalem, Jerusalem, thou that stonest the prophets, I would have gathered you as a mother hen gathers her chicks, and ye would not. [see Matt. 23:37]

I love you, O Jerusalem. I weep over you, O Jerusalem. I long to draw you unto Myself. I long to pour My Spirit upon you. I long to reveal Myself to you as your Jehovah God — as El-Shaddai, as Jehovah-Rophe — and ye will not.

Oh, weep for My people. Cry day and night for the deliverance of My people. I will once again set them free. I will once again bring deliverance and peace. But I need someone to intercede, to stand in the gap, for them; I need watchmen for the house of Israel. Cease not to cry day and night for My house, My children. I am a covenant-keeping God. I will answer; I will deliver. I will perform all things that I have said — I will perform all My Word.

I have set thee as a watchman for the house of Israel. Cease not to pray; cease not to intercede. This is the burden of the Lord that I place upon you this day. Pray in the Spirit. I will show you things to come — mysteries — as you pray according to the Spirit's leading. You will be praying My will for Jerusalem. Oh, be faithful and diligent. There is much to be done.

Pray for Israel

My Word calling My people to pray for Israel is not going forth as it should today. It must go forth. I will put a fervency to pray for Israel in the hearts of My people when I am their first love. For when they fellowship much with Me, I can put that burning desire of My heart into them, into you. For it will not come in the natural, but it will come by My Spirit in those who seek Me with all their hearts.

You must call the Jews back to Israel from the four corners of the earth. You must break down strongholds that keep them from coming back to physical Israel, and break down the strongholds in their hearts that keep them from receiving Yeshua [Jesus] now. But first, I must break down those strongholds in your hearts, because many of you do not have a desire, a fervent desire, to pray for My people, Israel.

I say pray for the peace of Israel; pray for the peace of Jerusalem. Pray that the Blood of Yeshua be around My Land and around My City. Pray that My Chosen Ones will come back and that many come to know Yeshua. Take My Name and My Blood over their hearts, over them. And as you pray, the strongholds that have kept them from Me shall come down: even stubbornness and rebellion, rejection, anger and bitterness, dark traditions, and the veil over their eyes that has kept them under the Law to this day, instead of in the freedom of Yeshua.

Pray with a fervency and with My bowels of mercy that I will give you. Come to Me with a contrite heart, with a humble spirit, and with brokenness, so you will see the love I have for them, the desire I have to graft them back in. It is according to My will and purposes in these Last Days, for the days of the Gentiles will soon come to an end. And pray for the Messianic Jews, that they may continue faithful and strong, witnessing and standing in the gap for their brothers and sisters.

As you continue in prayer, I will send out the angels with censers full of prayers to break into their lives, that their blindness might be removed, that they might see and behold Me and know and receive Me, even this day. And you will prepare the way for many who at the very last moments, even seconds, even in My appearing, shall come into My Kingdom, even as the one thief was saved as we hung side by side on crosses. The glory shall be so great that in those last seconds their eyes shall behold Me, and they shall cry out, "Yes, Yeshua, I desire You. Save me! Save me!" So pray, O My beloved, pray, pray, and bring in this harvest. My heart aches for their return.

So few preach and teach that I am calling My people to pray much for the salvation of My people, Israel. It has been omitted, and it is a sin! Seek for My whole counsel and for My wholehearted desire to burn in your heart, that I may burn out the dross in your heart and mind. Lean on Me, not on your own understanding. Ask that by My Blood and in My Name you be set free from apathy, even deceitfulness and prejudice, so that by the power of My Spirit and the anointing, every yoke in you will be broken.

For you have thought, "It's really not important, it's not important to pray for Israel." But I tell you that it is important, so very important. I need you bound together, yoked together, with Me in unceasing prayer — fervent, effectual prayer — for the return of My people.

I tell you, you will not love Israel in the future if you do not learn from Me to love her now — with tears. That's the sad part; that's the sad truth that is not understood by so many, so many who do not and will not preach it now. They are afraid — afraid of man and rejection from man. But I tell you the way it will be in the future, when the spirits of darkness will twist and turn things around and put the blame for many things on Israel. Many will not want to love Israel, and many of My children will turn against her. You must love her now through Me and by My Spirit, as I plant My love in your hearts and open the eyes of your understanding. Then, when the world and the governments and the powers of darkness turn against Israel, you will stand with her because your roots will be deep down in Me, in My heart, in My Spirit, in My will and plans; and you will not change. And I will bless those who bless Israel.

I desire to bless you. So seek Me and see if I will not pour out blessings from My heavenly throne that will flow out from you to all peoples and to My people Israel, and you will have a genuine love for them because you have a passionate love for Me. And that love for Me will give you the deep understanding you need.

I say that you must ask of Me, and I will give you nations as an inheritance for you. So ask Me for Israel, and I will give her to you, for she is My special nation. She is very near and dear to My heart, for I weep over her and have been waiting these many years for her return. So as you pray for Israel, your prayers touch a very special place in My heart. I am doing many miracles there, and you will see Me do many more as I prepare for My very soon return. And multitudes of My Chosen People shall come into the Kingdom as you pray.

The Coming Great Shaking[31]

It will not be long before there will come upon the world a time of unparalleled upheaval. Do not fear, for it is I, the Lord, who am shaking all things. I began this shaking through the First World War, and I greatly increased it through the Second World War. Since 1973 I have given it an even greater impetus. In the last stage, I plan to complete it with the shaking of the universe itself: with signs in the sun and moon and stars!

197

But before that point is reached, I will judge the nations, and the time is near. It will not only be by war and civil war, by anarchy and terrorism and monetary collapses that I will judge the nations, but also by natural disasters, by earthquakes, by shortages and famines, and by old and new plague diseases. I will also judge them by giving them over to their own ways, to lawlessness, to loveless selfishness, to delusion and to believing a lie, to false religion and an apostate Church — even to a "Christianity" without Me.

Be Prepared for My Purpose

Do not fear when these things begin to happen. For I disclose these things to you before they commence, in order that you might be prepared and that, in the day of trouble and of evil, you may stand firm and overcome. For I purpose that you may become the means of encouraging and strengthening many who love Me, but who are weak. I desire that, through you, many may become strong in Me and that multitudes of others might find My Salvation through you.

And hear this: Do not fear the power of the Kremlin nor the power of the Islamic revolution, for I plan to break both of them through Israel. I will bring down their pride and their arrogance and shatter them, for they have blasphemed My Name. In that day, I will avenge the blood of all martyrs and the innocent ones whom they have slaughtered. I will surely do this thing, for they have thought that there was no one to judge them. Be, therefore, prepared, for when all this comes to pass, to you will be given the last great opportunity to preach the Gospel freely to all the nations.

In the midst of all the turmoil and shaking, and at the heart of everything, is My Church. In the heavenlies she has joined Me in one Spirit, and I have destined her for the throne. You who are My beloved, whom I have redeemed and anointed, you are Mine. I will equip and empower you. You will rise up and do great things in My Name, even in the midst of darkness and evil, for I will reveal My power and My grace and My glory through you.

Do not hold back, nor question My ways with you, for in all My dealings with you I have always in mind that you should be part of My bride and reign with Me. Do not forget that this requires a special discipline and training. So yield to Me, that I might do a work in you in the time that is left, for I plan, even during all this shaking, that the bride will make herself ready.

I Have Set My Israel

And in the midst of the nations on Earth, seething with unrest and conflict, I have set My Israel. Yes, I say, My Israel. Even though they walk in disobedience and transgression in the stubbornness of their hearts, divorced from Me, nevertheless, always remember that I made them enemies of the Gospel for the sake of the Gentiles. I, the Lord, I Myself blinded them and hardened them that Salvation might come to the Gentiles in fullness. Yet they are still Mine, beloved by Me with a tender and undying love. They are My kith and kin, and I love them. Shall I give them up for all that they have done to Me? says the Lord.

Yet I have surrendered them to sorrow, to anguish of heart, and continuous suffering, but I have never given them up. In all their affliction, I was afflicted, though I neither delivered nor saved them from death. Nevertheless, I have been present: I, the King of Israel, I have been present — although unnoticed and unregarded — in all their sufferings. There was no gas chamber, no massacre in which I was not present.

But now the time has surely come when I shall receive them, for I shall reveal Myself to them, and with astonishment they will recognize Me. For in the midst of these judgments, multitudes upon multitudes will be saved of the nations. You will hardly know how to bring the harvest in, but My Spirit will equip you for the task! And to Israel will

I also turn in that day, and I will melt the hardening that has befallen her. I will turn their blindness into clear sight and tear away the veil from their hearts. Then they shall be redeemed with heart-bursting joy, and it will become a fountain of new and resurrection life to the whole company of the redeemed.

Do not fear these days, for I have purposed that you should stand with Me and serve Me. Fear not, for I love you, and I will protect you and equip you. I, the Lord, will anoint you with a new anointing, and you will work My works and fulfill My counsel. You shall stand before Me, the Lord of the whole earth, and serve Me with understanding and with power. And you shall reign with Me during these days.

Do not forget, says the Lord, that I call you above all other things to be intercessors in My presence, that I might work those works through My servant that will glorify Me and be the means of bringing many to Myself.

Prepare the Way for My Chosen People

I am calling My prodigals [Jewish people] back from the farthest corners of the earth. But so many of you, My people, are like the elder son; for you are jealous and you have not the depth of that love relationship with Me such that you desire them back, and you do not fervently labor for that celebration, for that day that is coming when I shall graft them in again.

Oh, how I yearn for My prodigals to come back. I have loved you and will not change My love for you. But because I love you and because I pour My Spirit out upon you, I am calling you, My people, My beloved, to prepare the way for My dear prodigals, My Chosen People, to come back.

I am calling you to prepare the way by My Blood, by My

very Blood that I shed for them when they didn't know Me. It's that same Blood I shed for you, and I say, "Prepare the way." Oh, call them in the Spirit by your prayers — fervent prayers. Call them by your prayers to come back, for I have a great celebration awaiting them. Call them to the Holy Land, where I will wrap them in My arms, where I will again graft them in, where I have prepared that feast that I will have for them.

For I love you and I love them. And you, I am calling you to prepare them for that feast, when they will know I am their King, and they will receive Me into their hearts. And I will put My signet ring on their finger and My robe upon them and shoes upon their feet. Oh, prepare the way for them to know Me, to receive Me.

Oh yes, My people, pray those fervent, effectual prayers to prepare their hearts and draw them from the uttermost parts of the earth to Me. For I am the Holy One of Israel, and I will yet reveal Myself to them as you pray, as you pray by the power of the Spirit.

And the celebration — we shall all be at that celebration: you and they, as they come back. It shall be a glorious celebration, when the time of the Gentiles shall be fulfilled and the time to graft My Chosen People in is at hand. And it is so soon, so soon!

Be about My business, be about My fervent prayer business and see that your hearts are filled with My love for them. Oh, I will pour My love, I will pour My bowels of mercy into you. So shall it be in those who love Me and know Me and heed My call according to My Word.

For they fit mightily into My End-Time plans. Search the Scriptures and see how I will again establish them as My people. They shall come forth, as their hearts are prepared to be a highway to Zion, as I come for them this day and in the days to come.

So that is a part of the work I have called you to, My people. Oh, the singing and dancing and rejoicing we will all do together. It shall be such a glorious time when all the streets shall be full of rejoicing.

Do you not see it? Can you not hear it, can you not hear it? It is on My heart every day. Let it be on your heart that there shall be such rejoicing — Jews and Arabs and all of us together. We shall rejoice greatly! That is the day when mourning shall be turned into joy.

Pray My People Back to Me

Through your prayers, My desert shall be watered. Through your prayers, My People shall return unto Me. Listen! Listen! I have called you Gentiles forth. I have called you to pray My People back, back unto Me! Oh, what an honor I have given you. Oh, what an honor I have given you to pray with love for My People. They return because of your prayers, because of your warfare, because you never give up. My people, never give up! Oh, My heart of love goes out to you. My heart of love is what you pray with. You ask, and you receive love for My People, the Jews.

Oh, the hand of Almighty God moves because you pray for them. Yes, you shall see what this world has never seen. You shall see the return of My People to My land, the land where I grew up, the land where they rejected Me. They shall come back, and they shall acknowledge their Saviour, and their arms shall open wide to receive Me. Their hearts shall open wide, and I shall enter into the hearts of My People because you prayed.

I Will Bless Those
Who Stand by Israel[32]

Yes, I am gathering My people Israel back to their home-land before the end comes. There will be those who refuse to go, due to their circumstances, and they will die in the wilderness. There will also be those in My Church who refuse to hear this call in their hearts, and they will also die in the wilderness, spiritually. [see Esther 4:13]

Those who will stand by Israel, I will bless and multiply their barns; and they will have plenty to give in the days to come.

It has not been spiritually easy for many. Many of you have had multiple losses; but know this, that I have been there with you, and I have seen it all. I will replace and multiply what the enemy has stolen from you. Yes, I will multiply it back seven times more! says the Lord.

So be encouraged and know that I AM the Lord. I AM still on the throne, and I will keep My own. Those who continue to stand by Israel, I have placed under My special wings; and I will make sure that My blessings will continue over them, and that My mantle of plenty is over them.

Those who have lost the vision for this all . . . I will bring it back to you in a fresh way . . .

7. Remember the Children

The Bride in Action (III)

A Sign and a Wonder

My little children are like little seeds, and they shall sprout up and take on the wings of My Spirit, and I shall breathe on them and flower them. And I shall do a new thing in the earth with My little, tender, very young shoots. They shall be a sign and a wonder to all the earth. They shall bring great glory to Me, for many shall hear their songs and hear their tender words of love and their message of mercy — mercy their beloved, gentle, enfolding Jesus has for all the peoples and children of every nation and tongue.

Pray for My little children. Pray, for I shall protect them with My Blood and teach them in the cradle. Yea, in the womb!

Note: Children are tender, innocent, transparent before Jesus. He was speaking of very young children — up to 3, maybe 4, *at most* 5 years old.

Remember the Children

Remember the children! Pray fervently for them! War in the Spirit for them to be established in Me. For they are very precious to Me. They are treasures to Me, near and dear to My heart, and I have important plans to use them for My glory in these Last Days.

Yes, a small child shall lead them — weary, battle-worn, lost, maimed, sick and dying ones, adults — into My Kingdom. For I shall anoint their words — My words — which they shall speak with My power. I shall use children — fresh and energized and inspired with great expectation and trust in Me, with deep devotion to Me. For when children know Me intimately and have security in Me, their trust and confidence grow strong, very strong. And as they grow in Me and through Me, they will wax strong with boldness and courage, unshakable! So pray diligently; train and nurture them diligently. Pray much for parents, teachers, and those who work with them, to train children up in My ways, and see what I will do with children and youth who are Mine — who know Me as their HERO, CHAMPION, and FRIEND, a Friend who sticketh closer than a brother.

Even as I called young David, Samuel, Jeremiah, Mary, and many others at an early age, so I am calling young ones into My End-Time Army, to grow strong in Me and in the power of My might. They shall be among the simple and foolish things I will use to confound the wise. They will be visited and led by angels. They will have visions and dreams. They will know Me and believe in Me deeply. Teach them My Word and how to know and love Me intimately and reverentially, how to dwell in Me and be separated unto Me, how to have a daily secret closet of prayer, how to humble themselves before Me and resist the devil unto victory.

The battle, fierce and often heart-breaking, is raging for their very lives. Many are falling! Hordes of demons are warring against them, even through those in authority over them, of whom I say, "It would be better if a millstone be hanged around their necks and they be sunk in the sea." [see Matt. 18:6] But I have given you the weapons of warfare for victory, even My Blood and My Name, even the Sword of My Spirit, even weeping and travailing for their souls, to break the strongholds, chains, and powers of darkness over them and in them. Apply My Blood over them day and night, as they go and as they sleep, for it is My impenetrable protection over them, and over you.

Who will lay down their lives for My precious children, that they might come unto Me, and grow and wax strong in Me? Who, in love, dares to discipline them for righteousness' sake? See them as I do, for those who are Mine are of the Kingdom of Heaven. My arm is not too short to save them and use them for My glory, as you pray without ceasing. Then watch and see what I will do, even with the children who have truly come unto Me.

Teach Them of Me

See why it is so important to train up a child in Me? For when they are teens and young adults, they will hear the rumble of the enemy and they will hear My still voice in their prayer closets! Yes, even My youngest can be taught to resist the enemy and send him fleeing with My Son's Blood and in His Name. They may be young and innocent, but they are, oh, so teachable.

Even the children shall the enemy army devour unless you teach them of Me and of secret prayer and of My promises of love and protection and how to use the sword of the Spirit of Truth and all parts of My armor, as soon as they can begin to talk. Let their third word be a call upon My Son's Name, Jesus!

8. The Rapture of the True Church

Which Christians are Going?

Which Christians Will be Left Behind?

You Expect to Be Carried Away in My Rapture[33]

My world, go unto thy God, and away from the world and the appetites thereof. Go ye out of the midst and be thou clean, ye vessels of the Lord. For strangers have entered in amongst My flocks and have destroyed My Life essence, so that I am once again forced to stand without and knock.

O foolish people and a people without hope, how quickly would I return unto thee if thou wouldest return unto Me, saith the Lord thy God. But thou must fully turn from thy gods of men, of brick or of stone, and even all thy lusts of greed and pride, of power, of authority. Even all of thy good and righteous works are as filthy rags before My holiness. Ye expect to be carried away in My Rapture to inherit heavenly homes for which you have not worked, have not changed, have not earned. How thinkest thou that I could accept into the pure heavens those that lie, that cheat and steal? For within thou art not changed. Thou hast not entered into a covenant with Me. Thou hast only taken a name upon thyself, that of Christ, yet ye live not the life thereof. Therefore there is no change wrought within, and thou art not fit for a heavenly abode.

Flee out of Babylon, that great religious city full of harlots, and come unto One, even the Good Shepherd Himself.

And He will feed you and water you as a shepherd feedeth his flocks; and ye shall lie down, and none shall make you afraid. Come away from the voices of thy many teachers unto the still, small voice of the Comforter, the inner Teacher, Who should guide you into all truth. Why do you spend your money for that which is not bread, and your labor for that which satisfies not thine appetite? Serve yourselves of Me and delight thyself with fatness. Even come and share My delicacies in the secret place of the Most High, and there I will teach, and I will lead, and I will guide thee with Mine eye.

But you are blind; but you are deaf. But you are complacent. Go ye out of the midst and be separate and pray; yea, cry aloud unto God and mourn that He would change thee from within before it is too late for thee to be carried away in Him. For the time is short, My people. There is not much time left. Therefore, seek Me with all your heart *alone,* and I shall hear, and I shall answer thee. Come away from thy many teachers unto One, thy inner Teacher, that shall take of the Father and show it unto thee, and He will bring to thy remembrance those things I have said unto you. My peace I give unto you. But few are in such a place as can receive it. Peace I would give unto you as a deep flowing river, but you will not come fully turned unto Me.

Cast away the little idols in your hands that separate you from My will. Yea, come empty-handed and alone into your prayer closet and there spend many hours alone, and you shall find I will meet you there, even as I have promised. But I am cast out from your fine church houses for the popular beliefs of today which damn the soul instead of liberate it! I am not to be found in your churches, My people, but in the aloneness closet of your heart, *if* you would but diligently seek for Me there.

O come, O My people. O stay and seek and listen to hear if I would respond unto thee. O come and let Me change thee from within. There is no power within thyself to change that moral degradation ye see. There is no power in any church or any knowledge known of men to free thee from thy chains of self and pride. Only I have the keys to unlock thy prison doors. Therefore, come to Me all ye who labor and are heavy laden, and I will give thee rest. Take MY yoke upon thee — become yoked in membership only to Me — for I am meek and lowly of heart, and ye shall find rest unto your souls.

But they who look unto men and believe in their promises never come into My rest, but are as the troubled sea and can never rest but are constantly full of turmoil. The water getteth deep, the troubles increase upon the world of woe. Soon all shall be much worse. Who shall guide you in the days to come when your preachers are taken away?

My people, though you have many shepherds, ye are as a flock untended, for grievous wolves have taken My flocks from unfaithful shepherds and have devoured them and stolen from them and lied to them. And thus are they secretly brought down to Hell and know not their situation until it be too late. Be not as they, but come away and seek Me in My Kingdom — not through knowledge but by the Spirit — and come into My Covenant with Me; and those that are Mine shall become one with you, as I am One with them.

Fear not the loss of reputation or of all things. For what good is it to a man if he gain the whole world and yet lose his own soul? If you would truly follow Me, ye must lay down your life, your reputation, all your fine things, to become lowly and meek like unto Myself. I would have you without pride and ego. You would have you full of both! Let Me cleanse you of all that offends to make you ready to receive heavenly joys. For nothing enters this heavenly abode that defiles in any way the holy atmosphere. I cannot allow any of Hell to enter here.

All that come are pure and clean from the spots, stains, and wrinkles of the world. Their hands are clean, their hearts are clear, and they worship before only One, even Jesus. And

I cannot withhold this heavenly abode from those who have not stood afar off from Me, even those who have come away alone unto Me to pray, to sup with Me, to learn to become "Oned" with Me. Thus are My children begotten unto higher realms of understanding, not ever learning but never growing, as those whom men teach. And these, My pupils, do come to the mountain of the Lord's house, and do learn My ways and walk in My paths and share in My glories and wealth of wisdom and understanding.

All that I promised thee thou wouldest receive if only thou wouldest come away unto Me alone in thy prayer closet, there to pray for changes, to pray for greater understanding. Go not to men to be taught, but come unto the Author of thy salvation, Who is also the Finisher of thy faith, *if* you will allow Me to continue that work begun in you when you first came humbly to Me for help.

There is no man that can save you; go not after them. Beware of them. If thou hast found that I am alive and glorious, come thou unto Me fully, and I will share My glory with thee. But if you insist on going to men — yea, here and there — I cannot help you, because as the prodigal you go far from Me. But come again and see that I will receive you unto Myself, but go not out again. Stay with Me. Let Me teach you alone. Give Me time to reveal to thee My secrets. Come away from thy worldly teachers — even all of Christendom! They are not one with Me by association. Only they who come alone to hear My voice and to learn from Me become one with Me. These I call My friends. And I can withhold nothing from them as they come alone seeking hard after Me. I change them from within and endue them with Spirit power to withstand the enemy; and they come to know My peace that passes understanding. Yea, they inherit My promises; they enter My Covenant; they become one with Me, even thy God, saith He that loveth thee and calleth thee again to come unto Me!

My Kingdom Is at Hand[34]

. . . . Be prepared for Me, for I shall come unto thee in a blinding splendor, and ye shall not be able to bear it if ye have been regarding the darkness about thee. Look above the present scene, for to dwell on the confusion of the world would unfit thee for the revelation of Heaven. You are not going to be here much longer, and no one spends time nor thought on what is soon to be left behind.

Abundantly have I blessed you; thy gratitude for this is fitting. But there are far more wonderful things that I am about to do for you, so keep thy heart free and thy mind stayed upon Me. The Great Revelation is unfolding, and the ushering in of My Kingdom is at hand. I would prepare thee. I have truth to give thee that is vital to this hour. Ye need to receive it now so that ye shall not be perplexed.

It shall indeed be a dark hour for the world, and humanity shall be enshrouded in a darkness such as in the days of the flood. This shall be an even greater darkness, and there shall be anguish and travail. But out of this shall come a new age of righteousness and of peace; and all creation shall struggle in travail until it be brought forth.

But I am lifting My chosen ones even now into a realm of glory and revelation. Yea, I am bringing forth a special unique creation. It shall be as Noah and as Lot, even the righteous remnant, which shall be delivered out of destruction.

For judgment must fall upon sin and all ungodliness. Evil must be purged and put away. But I will always have a witness, saith the Lord, and I will not forsake My people who put their trust in Me. The greater the judgment, the greater the deliverance; and the greater the darkness, the greater the glory. The greater the lie, the greater the Truth. . . .

This is the night of man's rebellion and disobedience. Ye are beginning to see the fulfillment of the second Psalm. But

211

in this night, the door shall be opened. It shall be opened by the Bridegroom. And they who are watching, and they who have maintained their lamps of witness, shall go in. Others shall see and shall desire to enter, but shall be too late!

See that thy witness not cease. Only as ye have a full supply of My Spirit can the fire of testimony be kept alive. THEY WHO HOLD DARKENED LAMPS COULD SCARCELY BE UNBELIEVERS; for the lamp is My Word. My Word without My Spirit can produce no witness. The fire is the witness, and the fire cometh never from the Word alone, but always from the Word and the oil of the Spirit. See that ye lose not the oil. When those who possess the oil have been taken away, where shall ye go to buy?

Be filled, My people, and be burning; for when I come, I shall come for the living, not for the dead. For the *living witness* I shall preserve, to carry the light over into the Kingdom Age.

Philadelphia Love
Can Unify the Body of Christ[35]

Now, I have brought you through this Church Age unto the age of the open door in Heaven for the glory of the Lord, as revealed to My servant John, My servant of love, and I offer to you this day the door of hope, the very door of the Philadelphia Church. There is controversy and competition between this great Philadelphia love, and that [love] of Laodicea for the greed of the world. Now I have offered to Laodicea My mercy and My grace. Yea, I have counseled her to buy of Me gold tried in the fire, yea, gold that perisheth not, and white raiment that she may wear to cover her nakedness and her poverty. She has said, "We are increased with goods and have need of nothing."

This is surely the attitude and the song of the sluggish

Christian today that walketh not after My will and My counsel. They do not know that they are naked. They do not know that they are blind. But I have offered to them now, even now, the eye salve which is the Holy Spirit anointing. This eye salve put upon their eyes will cause them to renew their vision again. They can behold their need. I cried to them to repent, for whom I love, I chasten and rebuke.

Oh, there is no comparison between the Philadelphia and the Laodicea Churches. Yet, they are both in My body. Those who have lived in Laodicean pleasure will have no burning lamp at the Rapture of the saints! . . .

Money and Pleasures Blind Many and Shall Cause Them to Go into The Great Tribulation[36]

Do you not see this, My children? Blinding things are money, pleasures, superfluous things, weights and cares of this life, which will cause many to be here in the Tribulation, and they will not escape by any means. Therefore, go forth and prepare yourselves and wash your hands in the pool of Blood that is behind the inner veil. . . .

Woe to the Dilatory Servant[37]

But there will come this thing, the signs of the times. And My dilatory servant, who will not prepare and will eat with the glutton and the drunken and say the Lord has delayed His coming, they will all be given a portion with the hypocrites. As you know, this is My Word; now speak It to everyone that they must prepare for Me. They must don their wedding robes — the white robes of redemption, of justification, of sanctification, and, yea, of glorification in its entirety. And

213

when this is all finished and My chosen ones have fully prepared themselves, I the Lord will break through and I will come. Now therefore, wait for Me; but wait not to prepare them to receive Me in the day that I shall come, saith the Lord.

God Will Soon Forsake Many, So Be Prepared for the Rapture[38]

Move in Me, and I will take you over the cliffs. I will take you over the mountains. I will take you up from the brush heaps and out of the sand piles. I will take you from the debris of human ingenuity and theologies that I have spoken to you about, that have become corrupt. It has become false psychology, false science. It has become so false that I have left it, saith the Lord.

Now I am getting ready to leave many churches. I am getting ready to depart from many homes. I will not send My angels into homes where I will not send My Blood. I will not send My Blood upon the household where they grieve Me and tempt Me with this stumbling block of television, where they center their minds on and view those obscene scenes and look upon them and let their children do so. I will remove My Blood! saith the Lord. I will remove My angel, saith the Lord, and thy prayers cannot stop Me then. Thy prayers cannot change Me then.

So thou hadst better pray now that thou also be changed to the fullest degree and be prepared for the Rapture. . . .

Warning to Refill Our Vessels
With Oil[39]

Those Who Hear the Bridegroom's Voice will Rejoice

Even as it was in the days of Elijah, yea, even in the past ages, many of the sons of the prophets knew and foreknew that Elijah would be translated — [yet] they did not see him when he went away. And behold, even now the sadness of such a time as this, that in these ages — even in this very hour in the time element of God's calendar — there have been many who have known about the coming of the Lord and have looked forward to beholding Him, who would be standing afar off. They would not be permitted to enter into that bridal party where all the prophets, who have been since the world began, were joined in the grand reunion. And even where John the Baptist will stand beside the Bridegroom, even Jesus, that he might declare himself that that is his joy to be beside the Bridegroom. "He that heareth the Bridegroom's voice will rejoice; and that is my joy," says John.

Now is the Time to Cleanse Ourselves

Now therefore come, My people, and enter your closets and hide yourselves, as it were, for a little moment until the indignation be overpast, for I am calling for intercessors now to come in and to fill up this age which is swiftly passing and will go faster than ever before. And the lightning shall come forth, yea, that He will send upon His intercessors who have waited for Him and who have cleansed themselves from all filthiness of the flesh and the spirit, perfecting holiness in the fear of God; for the hour is coming and will soon be past for people to cleanse themselves. And then shall come to pass that great and terrible pronunciation, yea, that will be said to them: He that is holy, let him be holy still; he that is righteous, let him be righteous still; he that is filthy, let him be filthy still. And so it will be that time will be no more.

So prepare thyselves against these great days of doom and degradation. Behold the bride in the 45th Psalm, and take the admonition with him to her as the queen in gold of Ophir, that she shall hear the voice of her Beloved. She will forget her own people and her father's house to follow Him who is leading her to the King's palace. And she shall be arrayed in raiment of needlework, and she shall have attendants, even virgins, according to Matthew the 25th chapter.

But lo, there will be one half of the virgin company who will not have oil in their lamps. Yea, there will be many turned out into darkness, weeping and knocking on the door of Heaven, who won't have oil. They did not have enough of a supply; they did not have that extra, continual flow of oil. . . . It is high time to accept this as a challenge and an index finger pointing to you, My children, to be prepared against that day of the doom of the five virgins.

Oh beware, saith the Lord, and become humble before Me and refill your lamps. Yea, refill with the Spirit of the Lord, as I have admonished by the apostle to arise and await and fill your lamps. Yea, and trim them and be prepared for the trumpet sound. Much confusion is in the air today. Many of My people who are lukewarm are sluggish, and they are not comprehending and discriminating into things that pertain to the inheritance of the saints in light. For the age that thou art now living in hath been the late age, the late age of light. Thou hast been duly warned to refill your vessels with oil.

God's People to
Stir Out of Their Sluggishness[40]

. . . . And will I not do more for this generation than I did for Sodom and Gomorrah — if thou will turn to Me and seek Me in the faith of Abraham, Isaac, and Jacob; the apostles of the Lord Jesus Christ; Paul, the apostle that was born out of due time; all of My leaders and multitudes of My people who are not only on the earth but in the heavens, that are seated there in the City of the Great King. Yea, they are there as spectators watching the scenes of Earth, watching the saints — whether they will be faithful, whether they will be able to overcome the antichrist that is coming against them. If they are not ready to come out of this, then they are going to suffer martyrdom!

Listen to My Word again. Yea, listen to It. . . . Every Bible student, every teacher of every Bible school, let the Word of the Spirit come and quicken you to reach out and receive It. Let Me send forth in thy way, for I am the Lord thy God. I am He that fainteth not.

Therefore My servants, My bachelors, My maidens, yea, all of My mothers, and all of the people all over this earth, hear this word: Arise from where you are and do not be so consumed with the things of the world. Be in one accord, all together, because I enjoy days of pleasure for you to fellowship and to glorify. And I want you to know that I'm standing in the fire of the Upper Room. I'm ready to pour the lightning out upon you with My latter rain accompanying. If you are not ready, I will send it to the heathen. I will send it across the seas. I will send it everywhere. You have the first chance today. But if there is not a great and mighty quickening, then **you will not be ready** when I shall come in the clouds with glory, in the twinkling of an eye, to catch away My beloved.

O hear Me, hear Me, My children. Awake even now, for it is time for you to awake and receive this mighty power of the Lord your God.

Wonders Will Come Forth[41]

Like a glow of summer sunset, so will the Lord come forth with His wonders. He will bring wonders at the very darkest hours of mankind. He will bring forth a recreation, a transformation, and a transportation.

BUT FIRST THERE MUST BE A TRANSFORMATION IN THE LIFE OF A PERSON THAT WILL BE TRANSLATED [Raptured]. This is the thing that is most important, saith thy God. Become transformed day after day, transformed by the renewing of thy mind — renewing why and how and what, with the Word of God, the Word that teacheth all these wonders, all of this inheritance of thine. . . .

I will, therefore, have you cleanse yourselves from all filthiness of the flesh and spirit, and perfect holiness in the fear of God. And in the fear of God have your conversation holy and righteous.

A Place for Preparation[42]

. . . . [There] is a spiritual dimension which I have come to order and to ordain that you might know this, that you might eat of the fruits of paradise in the Spirit, saith the Lord. There is a paradise spiritual and a paradise literal, and it will bring My people into a place to prepare them for the translation of the saints; yea, to come up to the realm of the unknown and the Lord, where they will see the angels and the archangels and saints of old; and there will be no sorrow, no weeping, no pain, no crying. For I the Lord God will wipe away all tears from their eyes. Yea, I will bring My people up. I have brought up a very few, but I will bring all the congregation — as many as will be dedicated and sanctified to the Master's use. . . .

Prepare for the Soon Coming of the Lord[43]

God's Stream of Light Shall Erase Man's Blindness

.... Remember the ten virgins who went out to meet the Bridegroom, and five were wise and five were foolish. The wise had burning lamps. The foolish had burning lamps, but the foolish took no oil in their vessels with their lamps, and their lamps went out on the way. They cried to the wise ones, who took extra vessels of oil — a custom in those days because the journey was too long and the lamp was small and contained only a small measure of oil. And so it was that the wise stored away the oil, as I want you to do.

Prepare for the Soon Coming of the Lord

I want you not to be satisfied with a status quo and have a mere single infilling, but get closer to God. Remember that in Ephesians the Lord is speaking to you about elevation, being lifted up. He said to be filled with the Spirit; be not drunk with wine wherein is excess, but be filled with the Spirit. And did He not also command that you sing psalms and spiritual songs? What did He mean by spiritual songs? He meant to sing in other languages as the glory of the Lord is come down.

It is the time of the sea of birds, and My dove bride is making herself ready now to receive Me when I call. But alas, the foolish ones, who have not kept their lamps burning and their oil replenished, shall go out into the darkness where there is weeping and wailing and gnashing of teeth in that Great Tribulation!

Therefore, beware and prepare, for the coming of the Lord draweth nigh, and no man knoweth the day nor the hour, neither the angels in Heaven. But the Father God is the One who knows, and the command of our Lord Jesus was to watch and pray. He may come at any time.

The four watches were set for certain events in that time. He spoke of coming any time, even if it meant the fourth watch. The Lord has been delayed by the neglect of His people to pray and to prepare for His return. But now they are coming up and seeking the glory of the Lord. They are crying out to Me and preparing themselves for the last lap of the journey.

So rejoice with Me, O children of God. Rejoice with one another, O people of the Lord, even the people of the Lord of Abraham. Whether thou be Jew or Gentile, yea, whether thou be bond or free, whether in prison or out of prison, these words will find lodging in your heart; and you shall prepare from this day forward to receive My glory, which shall come any moment that you open your heart to Me. For behold, I stand at the door and knock, and if any man hear My voice and will open the door, I will come in to him and sup with him and he shall sup with Me. You shall not be like the person, even the lover of the Song of Solomon, who would not get up in the night to open to her beloved. She said, "I have washed my feet, I've removed my shoes, I've taken off my robe, I am in bed, I am comfortable, I'm well satisfied." But the lover kept knocking and knocking. Soon he disappeared, and when she arose she could not find him. The only thing left was the fragrance of his presence. . . .

Those Filled with Oil of the Spirit Will Produce This Glory[44]

Now, before this glory can fully appear, the high priesthood of the Lord Jesus must be completed in Heaven, and simultaneously, the priesthood of His saints upon the earth, as recorded in the first chapter of Revelation when John cried out that He hath redeemed us, washed us in His Blood, and made us kings and priests unto our God. This is the heritage of the people of the Lord who qualify, who will keep their lamps trimmed and burning and filled with the oil of the Spirit that will produce this glory.

And there as you see in the 25th chapter of Matthew where the virgins [are], even the ten virgins who were the accompaniment of the bride of Christ — five of these were wise and five were foolish. The foolish ones did not have the supply of oil. And this is an admonition and a warning to all of My people now to keep your lamps trimmed and burning. But keep a supply — even an extra supply of oil — that at any moment you can be like John, who was immediately in the Spirit when he was called from the upper regions; you can immediately enter into the glory of the Lord.

And just that way will come the Lord for His people to rapture His Church, and you must be prepared to immediately be translated [Raptured]. . . .

Many Have Missed This Calling and Will Go Through the Great Tribulation[45]

. . . . Send out this truth: that I am the Word that was in the beginning with God and became flesh. Yea, I became flesh, and now I am glorified, that My people shall go through the same process that I went through, figuratively, and they shall come into My presence as they follow Me to the Cross and they are identified with Me in My crucifixion, in My burial, and in My resurrection, of the means of baptism and the glorious outpouring of the Spirit.

The Call of the Bride

I will know you after the flesh; for that is why I came in the flesh — to know you after the flesh. I took not on the nature of the angels, but I took on the seed of Abraham that I might destroy the works of him that had the power of death; that is, the devil. But I also came that I might yield to you

221

and you yield to Me. I have yielded Myself to you in blessing and glory. I have not submitted Myself to your dominion, but I have yielded My Word. Yea, your spirit ravished My heart. Your spirits have come and called upon Me and rejoiced, and not it is just as the bride and the bridegroom, for I am also preparing to receive My bride to Me.

And this bride must be separated to Me wholly, undefiled. Yea, My love, My dove, My only one. Who shall be greater than the bride? Is not she the one that looketh forth in the morning; yea, that is as fair as the moon, and as clear as the sun, and as terrible as an army with banners? That is the one that shall ride with Me on white horses!

Many Have Missed This Calling and Will Go Through the Great Tribulation

O that My people knew this day how far they are away from this place! So many of them claim it and preach it and rejoice in the hope of it, and that shall never do, because they have never donned the very armor of the Lord, the apparel of the Holy Ghost, the baptism with its magnitude and its glories and its personal powers. They have not donned this very white robe. They have not been altogether spotless. [They will go through the Great Tribulation.] . . .

But not so with you, and not so with others — **if** ye shall hear My voice this day. You shall now begin to show forth the white-robed ministry: white, pure as Heaven itself, unspotted. Do not condescend to flesh. Do not contemplate in those dimensions, but be in the Spirit. . . .

A Warning to Those
Not Ready for the Rapture[46]

. . . And now is the time to tell My people to prepare to escape this thing [the Great Tribulation]. Did I not say to My children to pray always that ye may be accounted worthy to escape all these things and to stand before the Son of Man?

O fear not to declare it. Yea, by all My ministries declare that My coming is at hand and that the five foolish virgins will not go into the Marriage Supper. But there will be weeping and wailing and outer darkness and gnashing of teeth when the Great Wedding is on, when it is spread out, when it is in full sway. Then shall the King see that a guest has come that has not on the wedding garment. This is the parable that I spoke through My servant Matthew and others about this great consternation, that some will come right up to the hour of the Rapture and right up to the hour of being caught away, and because they have indulged in foolishness and in jesting and joking and television filth — yea, television scenes corrupted by Hollywood and satanic forces — even these will NOT go with Me. And I have foretold it.

Yea, I have prepared this escape, and that is by the great moving of the Rapture, and that will come suddenly. No man knoweth the day nor the hour.

God's Message to the Church at Ephesus
Applies to the Church Today[47]

. . . . Oh, pray ye that your flight be not hindered, that you may rise above the enemy now, that you may be counted worthy to overcome and to stand before the Son of Man in that day when you shall declare His love and righteousness to His happy people who have walked with Him in the pureness of mind, spirit, soul, and body, by the Spirit of the Lord and by the Blood of Jesus Christ.

Christ, the Ark of Safety[48]

Now therefore, be quick to hear Him and to obey that which He speaketh unto thee, and He will manifest Himself unto thee in ways that thou knowest not. He will appear to thee in the lonely hours, in dreams in the night. When troubled waters come, He will make Himself known as the great Ark of Safety, yea, the Ark of Prayer, and the Ark of Praise. He will make Himself known to you as the Ark of Refuge that Noah had, and as the Ark of Communion that Moses, Joshua, and others even today have had.

See that ark where the mercy seat was set upon it, and the cherubim (one at either end of the ark), and the Lord who promised, saying, "I will commune with you from above the mercy seat." He will meet you there. For all this is a type of Christ, in His death and burial and in His resurrection glory. And even as it was manifested in the rod of Aaron to bring forth a dry stick, even into the great truth of the resurrection — and quickened — that word is yours today.

You can live in that quickening so much that when the Rapture of the Church comes, you will be ready. *There will not be any time to prepare at that quickening sound!* And this is come to give you a warning of the time to prepare for the greatest event this world has ever seen. . . .

God's Message to the Church at Ephesus Applies to the Church Today[49]

. . . . Throughout the past 6,000 years the Lord God hath worked fervently among His people to bring to perfection those whom He had called in each age. . . . Remember ye not that He has spoken to you of His returning, that He would come in a moment, in a twinkling of an eye, at the last trump? The trumpet would sound and the Lord Himself would descend with a shout, with the voice of the archangel, and He would come to rapture, quicken, to catch away, *those who are prepared to meet Him.* . . .

A Warning
Concerning the Five Foolish Virgins[50]

Yea, tell My people about Chapter 25 of Matthew, where the five virgins that were foolish took no oil in their vessels with their lamps. Their lamps had gone out; their light had diminished. The five wise ones had burning lights because they kept the Word of the Lord in them, because they depended upon the principles of righteousness and the Word of God.

And the foolish virgins were doing what many ministers today are doing — relying on past experiences. They feel they only have to come to God and get forgiveness, and they make of it a light thing, as Samson did. But they shall not prosper in such things. Show them very clearly that at the rate they are going, they will NOT be ready to meet the Lord. And that is the ultimatum!

Transfiguration of My People
Should Come More Abundantly[51]

. . . . Oh, that ye would see this and prepare for it and take heed to all that I have spoken in this message, even now. And yea, that **ye should be ready** to be translated [Raptured] out of the world into the glory of the ages and with the triumphant Church with her Lord and Saviour, Jesus Christ, throughout eternal ages, saith the Lord.

9. How Much Time is Left?

Heavenly Visitors[52]

It was hard for me to fall asleep last night. I prayed a lot. When I finally fell asleep, I had a dream. I was in a valley with mountains around it. Someone yelled at me, "Run and hide! Rain is coming!" I thought, "I'm not afraid of the rain." I looked around and could not see anyone. Then I heard peals of thunder! A powerful bolt of lightning passed right by me! Out of it came two beings.

They asked if I was afraid. I said "Yes." They asked if I knew who they were. I said "No." They said, "We are heavenly beings." Their clothes were white as snow. They had eyes that were penetrating. There was a light in them so bright I could hardly look at them. Their hair was white as wool, and it was long, going down their backs. One of them had a book, and the other had an inkwell attached to his belt and a large pen in his hand. There was an eraser on one end.

The one with the pen said, "I was sent to complete the Book of the Gentiles." . . . He opened the back of the book and counted out four remaining blank pages at the end. "When these are filled," he said, "the Book of the Gentiles will be complete. Then I will return to My people. Some of the names that are listed here will be erased. I will erase the names of those who have mocked God and tested the Spirit of Grace. I will replace them with other names."

I started to ask what the four pages meant, but before I

could ask the meaning, he thrust the pen into the inkwell, as though slipping a sword into a scabbard. As he did, there was such tremendous thunder and lightning that I fell down. Then I woke up.

Clouds in the Sky[53]

After I prayed, I went to sleep. While I was sleeping, I dreamed that someone was telling me, "Rain is coming!"

I looked around but saw no one. Suddenly there was thunder and lightning! A red cloud appeared, and in its midst were a hammer and sickle. In another direction there was another cloud, but with no unusual colors. Suddenly, a bright star appeared out of the cloud! Then the red cloud began to surround the cloud with the star and tried to capture it. At that time a white cloud appeared with great thunder and lightning! When it appeared, the red cloud was destroyed. Then two men appeared out of the white cloud. One had a face like the sun — so bright that you could not look at it. The other had a humble face and had a book in his hand. He opened it and said, "Look."

He began to count the pages of the book. There were only three and a quarter empty pages. Then he said, "It won't be long; be prepared! When these pages are filled, God's grace will leave the Gentiles. Draw closer to Me now more then ever, and be holy because hard times are coming."

Then the man with the book said, "Look to the right." When I looked to the right, I saw a beautiful garden filled with all kinds of flowers, but none of these were flowers I had ever seen. Then I woke up.

A Dream[54]

On the 6th of November I had a dream, and then as usual I prayed and said, "If this dream is of You, Lord, let me dream it one more time." Then on the night of the 7th, God gave me the dream once again. In my dream I heard a great commotion, and as I looked, I saw a black cloud coming. . . .

Suddenly, I saw the black cloud disappear. Then two men dressed in shining clothes appeared. They were of gigantic size — because I remember I could not see their heads too well — and they both spoke with thundering voices: "Do not fear. Christ is the Victor." Each of them had a book in his hands. The books were covered with gold thread, and they were both the size of a table. Then these two men put the books down on a great table, and both spoke to me, saying, "Open, and read!"

I opened the first book, and I was told, "This is the Book of Life." The man on my left said, "Whoever finds his name in this book will be saved!" Then he said, "Open the second book!" The words "Book of the Gentiles" were scrawled on the second book. Then I began to turn page after page, upon which I saw all kinds of different names written. And so I reached the end of the book, where I found that there were one and three quarter pages left blank, unwritten. Then one of the two men said to me: "When the total number of the Gentiles is completed, the writing in this book will be finished. At that time, what I have shown you will happen: Then the beast will try to do battle against the holy. Remember what I tell you: Be prepared, live a holy life, and do not think that you have much time to live on this earth! Jesus is soon returning!" . . .

Yet Seven Days![55] . . .

The Lord would say to thee: Prepare for the coming days of trial and hardship. Prepare for the day of My judging the world. I am coming down, and I will speak. For a long time I have been silent. The world has not heard My voice. They have heard the voices of My prophets, My intercessors, and My singers, but I warn you, get ready to hear MY VOICE!

You will hear My voice in the clouds, in the thunder. It won't be normal thunder; it will be thunder on a cloudless day. You will hear the belly of the earth roar as the earth shifts and moves at My coming. It will be a fearful time, and the sinners shall tremble in great fear. For they shall know that I am God!

"Yet seven days! . . ." That is what I said to Noah. [Genesis 7:4a]

And I say, I will do nothing but I will reveal it to My servants, the prophets. [see Amos 3:7]

Sodom: Before I destroyed Sodom, I told Abraham what I was about to do. [see Genesis 18:17-22]

Nineveh: I warned Nineveh of impending overthrow in forty days. [see Jonah 3:4]

Jerusalem: I wept for Jerusalem because I saw its coming destruction. [see Luke 13:34-35; 19:41-44] Before the Roman Army destroyed Jerusalem, I allowed great persecution to come upon the early Church in the Holy City, so that they would be scattered all over the [regions of] Judea and Samaria. [see Acts 8:1] This is what saved their lives.

My people did not want to leave Jerusalem. They had read the prophecies that had spoken of My return on the Mount of Olives, and they were daily expecting Me to come back. [see Zechariah 14:4]

They did not want to go even as far away as Galilee, lest I would return while they were gone. Many of them had been on the Mount of Olives when I ascended to Heaven.

They remembered the promise of the angels, "Ye men of Galilee, why stand ye gazing up into Heaven? This same Jesus, which is taken up from you into Heaven, shall so come in like manner as ye have seen Him go into Heaven." [Acts 1:11]

They expected to see My return in their lifetime. But I knew I would be delayed, so to save them from slavery and death by the Romans, I sent them from the destruction that was coming on the city.

Today again, many shall leave their cities. Persecution, sin, crime, pollution, high taxes, economic collapse shall drive them out. And some shall go because they have heard My voice telling them to go. The wise ones are selling out and moving now. The not-so-wise will leave later, but they will not be able to sell. And last of all, the foolish shall stay until it's too late and lose their lives! Obey the voice of the Holy Spirit when He tells you to come into the Ark!

First you will see the political and the religious upheavals. Then you will see the upheaval of the earth as I come down, bringing retribution. This coming judgment will destroy whole cities!

Believe Me, on that day you won't have time to pack up. You won't be able to return into the house to get anything [see Matthew 24:16-17] because the earthquake will destroy many houses; and what the earthquake doesn't destroy, the fires will; and what the fire doesn't destroy, the floods will!

So hasten to come into the Ark!

"Yet seven days! . . ."

Seven is the perfect number. It will come in the perfect time, the appointed time! And nothing shall hinder Me. The gross sins of the people, the murder of the innocents, the perversion of the sodomists, the blasphemy of the rebellious to My face, will all STOP in one moment of time!

I am coming down! The earth shall know it! The mountains shall cleave asunder.

Yet seven days!
It's time for the move.
I give you just enough time to get ready now.
Come into the Ark!

No More Time

There is no more time, there is no more time, saith the Lord God. It is soon coming: There will be no more time to call upon My Name, no more time to seek My face, saith the Lord God! For we're running out of time, we're running out of time! I have created time for man to come to Me, but man has gone his own way and has spent that time upon himself, saith the Lord God.

Terrible times are coming, terrible times are coming to this nation, to this area, saith the Lord God; and I am raising up a few that will come unto Me and do My bidding, yea, My bidding. And I will send them forth to do My works.

They are not hearing it the way they should from the pulpit, saith the Lord God. They are not hearing it from the people that I have called Pastors. And My anger is waxing hot, and I am provoked by the things of the world that are in the Church, saith the Lord God.

Yea, and it is soon to come, so very, very soon to come. You are living in the very last of the Last Days, and there are only a few days left according to My way of numbering, saith the Lord God.

Yea, terrible times are coming, terrible times are coming — soon to come to this area, soon to come to your very own assembly, saith the Lord God — and I am preparing you for this. Stay close to Me; seek My face daily and pray. For it is I, and I alone, Who is guiding you. I am doing it, saith the Lord God, so stay close.

Pay no attention to the things around you. Pay no attention to what man says, but listen to My voice. Seek it, seek My voice. Knock and I shall open the door for you, saith the Lord God, for this is soon to happen, so very soon. Watch and see, My people. It is soon to take place!

It is The Time of My Visitation

These days, these times, are quickly coming to a close. Time shall be no more in the sense that you have always known it. Time will have slipped away, and we will be in the "hour" of God's timing. Things will happen with a swiftness, and all will be according to My divine plan and order. The hour is the time of My visitation. It is the exact time that I will bring to pass all that I have spoken in My Word concerning the last times. I work according to seasons and times. The hour is the time of My appointment. It is the conclusion; it is the consummation. It is the ending. Even the birds of the air know the times and seasons, but My people know not. They are like an ostrich in the wilderness!

Wake up! Look around you and run to Me. Cry out unto Me; cry mightily unto your God! Cry out in desperation, for soon, *soon* I come with an outpouring of judgment on all sin and unrighteousness! Come, come while there is still time! I call to you. Come into My arms of love. Forsake all and come with all of your heart. Hold nothing back. In doing this, you will have nothing to lose and nothing to fear. Come, come with all of your heart.

10. A Final Exhortation and Warning to ALL Christians

The Hand that Wrote on the Sky[56]

In my dream, it was as if my family and I were in a garden and we wanted to pick flowers. We were all looking around, trying to see which flowers were the most beautiful. I looked toward the sky. As I looked at the sky, I saw the head of a man and the hand of a man. I continued to look, and I saw the hand beginning to write: "Tell the people not to believe that what I have said are fairy tales and untruths. The day of terror is fast approaching, and it is close. I will not let one word that I have said go undone."

As I was reading what the hand had written, two men dressed in white suddenly appeared. They positioned themselves — one on one side of the head and the hand, and one on the other side. One of the men began to speak: "Tell the people to prepare, for the day of terror will soon be upon them. I will have mercy on those who today obey Me, those that depart from sin and draw closer to Me. I will give victory to those that will obey today." The second man spoke, saying the same words. Then everything disappeared, and again I was aware of my surroundings. . . .

Letters to the Churches[57]

I had gone to bed early — about 8:00 P.M. I woke up between midnight and 1:00 A.M. I got up and prayed, and then went back to bed. I dreamed that there was a lot of turmoil outside, and I kept hearing everyone yell, "Jesus is coming! Jesus is coming!" I looked out and saw a very large red cloud. When I looked at it, its outer edges could not be seen. As I continued to look, I saw a tall man come out of the cloud. He was so tall that although his feet touched the ground, I could not see his head. Rays of light began to explode out of the man. When one would pass by me, I would fall to the ground. I could not look at him with my eyes because he was too bright.

He then began to hand me letters; they were addressed to certain churches. I knew that these must be American churches because I did not recognize the names as being Romanian. The first letter said, "My people who are discouraged and beaten by the storms, many who have let themselves be beaten by the enemy — stand up! Cry out before God, that He may save you!"

The man kept coming and giving me more letters with names of churches of different denominations, and also independent churches. He gave me very many papers. Then he said to me, "When you finish taking these papers where you are supposed to, you will see something that you have never seen before."

There was thunder and the voice spoke again: "Tell all My people to pray and to repent. The days have been shortened because of all the iniquities. My people, repent, because the days are numbered."

I began to see the days passing by, but whenever the ray of light would pass by me, I would fall. The days were passing so quickly that I could not count them.

The voice spoke again: "Tell My people that I tried to wake them up through powerful storms, fires, floods, and earthquakes, but even then they would not wake up. This is why I will pour out My wrath when they least expect it."

The angel gave me a scripture, Joel 2:12-13: "Now therefore, says the Lord, Turn to Me with all your heart, with fasting, with weeping, and with mourning. So rend your heart and not your garments. Return to the Lord your God, for He is gracious and merciful, slow to anger, and of great kindness; and He relents from doing harm."

After these things, the cloud and the angel began to fade away.

When I awoke, I was wet with sweat.

The Black Army[58]

It was getting dark. Then suddenly it turned pitch black! It was as if the whole world had gone dark at that moment. All the people were in a frenzy! They became disoriented, and some were even screaming. After some time, we heard the sound of an army approaching. Soon we saw them coming out of the black mist. All were dressed in black, except one; that one seemed to be their leader. He was dressed in a red robe with a thick black belt over his waist. On his head he had a sign. As I looked, I saw that in his hand he held the same kind of sharp spear as everyone else in his army.

"I am Lucifer!" he exclaimed. "I am the king of this world! I have come to make war against the Christians!"

It looked as though all the Christians were huddled together in one big group. Some began to cry when they heard this. Others began to tremble, while some just stood without saying anything. Lucifer continued to speak: "All of those that want to fight against my army and think they can be victorious, go to the right. Those that fear me, go to the left."

Only about a quarter of the group stepped to the right. All the others went to the left. Then Lucifer ordered his army: "Destroy those on the right!"

The army began to advance and quickly surrounded the Christians on the right. As they began to close in on us, a powerful light appeared and encircled us. Then, an angel of the Lord spoke: "Take out your swords and fight! Defend yourselves and be victorious over the enemy!"

"What swords?" a man in the group asked.

"The Word of the Lord is your sword," the angel answered. When we understood what the angel meant, we began to quote verses from the Bible. Then suddenly, as if we were one voice, we began to sing a song. Our voices thundered so loudly that the dark army began to retreat in fear. They did not have the courage to come against us anymore.

Lucifer, then filled with rage, turned to those on the left: "You, who all of your life have been trying to please two masters — because you could not stand against me, I have the power to destroy you."

He then ordered his army to attack. It was a total massacre! The ones on the left could not defend themselves. One by one they all fell. This killing seemed to go on for a long time. After a while we could actually smell the stench of the dead.

"Why could they not be protected also?" someone asked.

The angel answered: "Because all their life they have been lukewarm. Because of their hypocrisy, the true church has been blasphemed. They have brought disrespect to the Word of God. They were not clean."

As we continued to look, we saw the sun coming over the

horizon. The black clouds began to break up; then they disappeared. Only one was left — on which Lucifer and his army stood. Lucifer looked at me, shaking his fists, and said, "I will destroy you, even if I have to throw my spear at you from here!" Then that cloud disappeared too. . . .

"I Never Knew You"

Look for Me in unexpected places and people and things. Look for Me in the weak and lowly, the hurting and despised, for I am there. But you shall not see Me if you are high and lifted up. You will not think to look for Me there, for your eyes and heart will be set to see only that which is lovely and pleasant and tasty and alluring. You will walk past and overlook the despised and weak. You will abhor the plain manna, and you will lust after that which satisfies the cravings and comforts and esteem of men.

You are so blinded and hardhearted that you don't even see Me. You have forgotten that I was despised and rejected of men, a Man of Sorrows, acquainted with grief, and you hide your faces from Me and esteem Me not. How blind you are; how cold-hearted and indifferent to the genuine needs of others! And you say you know Me? Is it not according to how you want to know Me? What a rude awakening you will have on that day when I come for My own and you hear the words, "I never knew you"!

Come, come and humble yourselves before Me now. Examine yourselves now. Let My Word search your heart and try your thoughts and ways. Repent of your sins and cry out for My mercy, for I will freely forgive and gather you unto Myself.

I love you. Turn, turn from your self-seeking, self-contained, self-controlled, and prideful ways. I will come to you and lead you in the way of humility, mercy, and meekness.

It is Who and What I am. It is life and light. You will overlook Me and pass by — and actually despise Me — if you will not answer My call of love to your heart.

Meet Me in the plain place of prayer, everyday, to seek and know Me; and your eyes and ears will be opened, as you repent and turn to Me in humility, willing to forsake all other loves and ways.

[Not everyone that saith unto Me, Lord, Lord, shall enter into the Kingdom of Heaven; but he that doeth the will of My Father which is in Heaven. Many will say to Me in that day, Lord, Lord, have we not prophesied in Thy Name? and in Thy Name have cast out devils? and in Thy Name done many wonderful works? And then will I profess unto them, I never knew you. Depart from Me, ye that work iniquity. (Matthew 7:21-23)]

Be Very Careful
Some Saints Lost Everything — Even Heaven![59]

In these Last Days you will be tested in every way possible, for Satan will seek to cause you to lose your reward. You have wondered why I have permitted these very great trials. They are even like the trials of Job. Satan wants you to lose everything in the last hours that remain before I come for you.

So I warn you to be very careful! Many of My greatest saints lost everything in the very last hours and days of their lives. You have wondered how it could have been that someone who was so greatly used of Me could have fallen so deeply into sin in the latter part of their lives. Now you know. They were terribly tested and tempted by Satan, and in the end, died without honor and lost their great inheritance. SOME EVEN LOST HEAVEN!

So take care, My beloved one! Keep your eyes on Me.

Every day will become a testing day. Every day will become a day when you must stay very close to Me, because the devil is going around like a roaring lion, seeking to devour the saints in these Last Days. And if he can't get them to lose their Salvation, he certainly will do all he can to get them to lose their rewards.

So stay close to Me. Stay filled with love. And be honest with yourself. It is one thing to be honest with others, but it is another thing to be honest with yourself. That is a state which few attain unto. But if you are not honest with yourself, you cannot deal with the weaknesses in yourself which will rob you of your crown.

Eternal greatness is only obtained during your temporal life on Earth, through your godly response to the hours of trials and testings which you are going through even now.

I love you. You are My precious treasure. And on the Day of Judgment, all who have tried to ruin your character or destroy you will "know that I have loved thee," and they will be ashamed. Hold fast to your crown! Don't lose it in these last hours of fiery trials! If you overcome, "I will make you a pillar in the temple of My God, and you shall go no more out. And I will write upon you the Name of My God and the name of the city of My God, which is New Jerusalem, which cometh down out of Heaven from My God; and I will write upon you My new name." [see Revelation 3:12]

Choosing the Lie

The day of the dividing of My sheep is now. It is not in the future; it is not in the past. It is going on NOW. Those that will go on with Me will follow on, but there will be a cost. There was a cost that I had to pay to follow the leading of My Father. There will be a cost for you to follow that leading, but the reward is great for those who follow Me.

And those who choose to go by the wayside (even though they do think they are following the correct way), they are following the precepts of men — what men have taught them. They have twisted and perverted My Scriptures, and no one has risen up to tell them of their error and, yes, their gross sin.

These people will go into apostasy because they choose to believe the lie. They have the **delusion** upon them. It is their choice because I left the way open for them to come. But they choose to follow their own paths, or the leadings and lies of other men to whom I have not spoken — I repeat: to whom I have not spoken!

These men, too, may repent and follow Me. I will accept all My sheep who will follow Me. But the time of the division is at hand. And those who will not follow Me will be sadly disappointed when I come, for they will go into gnashing of teeth (as it says in My Word), and I will say, "Depart from Me, for I never knew you."

So I'm asking you to follow Me. This is the division of My sheep. The way may be rough and dark at times, but you will not be left on your own. I will come and make My abode with you, and My Father will make His abode with you. (You know that is in My Word also.) And I'm bringing those people who will follow Me — My sheep who will truly follow Me — I will bring them into union with Me. We will be one, as it says in My Word, as a husband and wife are one. We will be one!

This is the higher calling. This is for the sheep who now choose to follow Me at all cost to themselves — they will have this reward [oneness with the Lord]. It is the calling that I give to all My sheep, but only a few will choose it, and they will be satisfied because they will have Me, Myself.

Who Falls Away?[60]

It is in the hard places of life that I can prove you. Both you and I need to know just how pure and strong you are. The Holy Spirit is always, at all times, searching into the depths of My people through trials and testings, difficult situations and temptations, to examine the deepest areas of your soul, that all evil and hidden sins might be revealed. I am looking, most of all, for integrity in man.

This is a time of proving. Not all who fall away now are falling because they have suddenly been tempted and are thereby overcome. Most who fall away have never been pure from the beginning. It is like a limb of a tree. For years it looks strong and healthy. But when the storm comes, it is broken off and then the worms and rot are revealed, which were eating on the inside of the tree and destroying its strength and goodness.

Storms are coming! Terrible days of testing are now upon all the world, and My people will not be spared. You will see many limbs, even mighty "oaks," fall. You will be in shock, but know this is only the hour of proving and testing. Deep within many of the hearts of My children are the same spirits as those which Moses was attacked by through the children of Israel — spirits of quarrelsomeness, fighting, contention, rebellion, discontentment, conflict, false accusation. You will see churches, ministries, families and friends split up because these things have been there all the time; but the hour of testing will reveal them.

I will have you to know all of My purity, and to ask for it and claim it. But how can you do this unless you can see your need of it? Hence the hour of testing in your life, which reveals to you your imperfections and the "worms" which are eating at your soul to destroy it. You must see them before it is too late and the limb breaks off, or the mighty oak of your life falls!

Many Christians Will Fall[61]*

Many are those who sit neglectful, loving the world and the things of the world. Many seek the life of the earth, but they do not prepare themselves to meet the Holy One. Jesus is coming! Do not be lazy!

Terror and great pain is coming upon the earth! The devil will take upon himself power, and he will attempt to make war with the holy. But Christ, the Victorious One, will come and will save His people.

Proud men! — all those who pretend to be teachers, and never living the life; all those who say they worship Me, yet their hearts are far from Me. Says the Lord: I will make them part of the suffering, torment, and terror, that they may call upon Me, but I will not answer.

Those that today humble themselves and seek Me with a clean heart, in that day — the hard day — will be glad and will rejoice. The power of the devil will increase greatly in this country [America], and many Christians will fall in its chains because they have dishonored Me with their lives — in their pride, their arrogance, and their vanity — thinking they are holy and are worshipping Me, yet *never really worshipping Me.*

The winds and the storms that will begin against the Christians in this country will take many. **Those who remain standing will be very few!** Humble yourselves. Be holy. Seek Me more than ever, kneeling before Me often, that in the hard days I may save you, says the Lord.

*Used earlier, in chapter 2.

The Saviour Returns as Judge[62]

It was seven o'clock in the morning when I woke up. I still felt a little tired, so I stayed in bed longer to rest. Then I fell asleep and dreamed that I was in an American church service, when the building began to move violently. Because they did not know what was happening, the people inside panicked and quickly began to run out. I succeeded in walking out also, but with every step I tried to take, it seemed like I was sinking into the ground. I began to look around to find something to support myself with so I could walk. I heard a voice that said, "Look up, and see the heavens!"

I looked up, and as far as the eye could see, all the sky was blood red. Then I said, "Lord! What does this mean? Why is the sky red?" Then I remembered my father telling me that before the great war the sky turned blood red.

As I stood looking toward the sky, a cloud suddenly appeared. Three men came out of the cloud. The middle One was dressed in shiny clothes and was of very great stature. He shined so brightly that I could not look at Him. The other two, one on His right and one on His left, were prepared for war. They had weapons in their hands that were pointed toward the inhabitants of the earth. Trembling, I asked, "Lord, what am I seeing? What does all this mean?"

When the One in the middle spoke, in a thunderous voice, all those around me were able to see Him. "I am Jesus Christ, who gave My life for you. Many of those whom I gave My life for, today dishonor Me, living in sin and things that are wrong. The honor and glory I deserve is not given to Me. For this I have no more mercy, but will soon return in glory and honor as Judge, to judge all the inhabitants of Earth. But first, I will judge those that carry the name of Christians, yet have tried to deceive Me. Because of them, My Name was and is dishonored and blasphemed before those that do not know Me."

"And about you," He said to me, "be awake! Be on guard more than ever, for you will go through many trials. Now the battle will begin to get harder. The devil is ready to begin war against the Christians; and I have allowed this."

Then the two men beside Him began to fire their weapons. A salvo of fire came out, lighting the sky, and it began to burn. The One who shone brightly stood in the midst of the flames, crying out with a loud voice, "Do not fear! All those who worshipped Me and have lived a clean life, those that suffered here on Earth, will have joy. For I am the One who will judge all of the nationalities of the earth. I will spare no one, and will not have mercy or grace for anyone. The day when I will punish and condemn is coming! I tell these things for everyone to hear. Hard days of suffering are coming to this place and over the whole earth. The hardships will be so great that the minds of man will not be able to understand it. It will be so hard that men will kill themselves. I will judge through torment, pain, and suffering; and will take revenge with great harshness for all sin. The Father has allowed Me to avenge My spilled Blood."

The other two began to fire their weapons again, but this time a blue flame came out. I fell with My face to the ground. The One in the middle yelled, "Get up! I want to show you the judgment of the people and the wicked. But **the hardest judgment will be received by the Church**, because they knew My Word and My power, but many of them dishonored Me, giving in to defilement, adulteries, wickedness, and [they] dishonored My Name before men who did not know Me. For this I am filled with rage, and I have been given the authority to take revenge against the inhabitants of the earth — those who have dishonored Me." The two that stood at either side of Him began to fire again.

A heavenly choir appeared that began to sing a song in the most beautiful splendor: "Jesus is alive. Jesus lives. Jesus is alive. Jesus reigns. Jesus is coming in glory. Jesus is no longer Saviour, but returns as Judge." I began to cry. I cried with tears of joy. I was in an atmosphere of incredible beauty.

The choir continued to sing as the two men with the weapons introduced themselves. The one on the right said, "I am the head of the Lord's Armies, Gabriel." The one on the left said, "I am Michael, the leader of the Lord's Armies. We are at the Lamb's command, and wherever the Lamb goes, we accompany Him." The choir continued to sing, and everything began to fade. I woke up with the words, "Jesus is no longer coming as Saviour, but as a Judge."

The Greatest Judgment Will Fall Upon My Church and My People![63]

My children, you are seeing and experiencing this earth rock and reel with the beginning of My judgments. And you have seen and heard of earthquakes more terrible than you have ever heard of before. But I tell you that the greatest judgment will fall upon My Church and My people! And it will come as a great shaking and rocking and explosion, and what it will accomplish is that it will separate. It will separate those who are truly following Me with all of their hearts from those who say they are apostles and say they are My followers and say that they love Me, but they do not! And it will be MORE SEVERE and MORE DRASTIC than you have experienced thus far!

I have called and I have called. My heart has wept and bled, and I have actually vomited when I have looked at My Church and that which they have dragged in — in My Name! And they do it in My Name! My Name they desecrate, My very Name and My very own temple! And they sit and they do not hear what I say to them. They do not hear!

245

But the separation will come, just as you have read about it in Matthew 25. The separation is very evident in the virgins: those who had oil and those who did not. In the sheep and the goats it was very evident who was on My side and who was really following Me, for lambs are the ones and sheep are the ones who follow Me. My children, do you not see that it is very evident that this is what I am doing now? I'm separating the wheat from the chaff. I'm separating. I am separating! And even though now you can hardly tell, it is the ones who are listening and the ones who are hearing My voice who follow. They will follow Me. They will follow the Lamb withersoever He goeth, and those are the ones who are hearing My voice, even now!

Will you be willing to follow Me all the way? Will you be willing in this world of materialism, in this world of get and grab and have, will you be willing to lay aside and come? For as the days grow darker, *and they will grow very dark,* only those who are truly hearing My voice and seeing Me — because they are searching for Me with all of their hearts — will be the ones who will have great joy in their hearts. And even though things will grow so dark, and the things of this world and the natural things will grow scarce, still, they will have that inner feeding and that inner fellowship; and their joy will be very, very great, and their lights will shine brightly. There will be no lack of oil in their vessels, because even now they are buying and they will not sell. They will not sell!

My children, I do not say this to frighten you, and I know you aren't frightened because you know what I'm doing. But anyone else hearing this will be very frightened. But do not be afraid, because I call you to Myself. I call you to love, I call you to peace, I call you to gentleness, I call you to plenty, because that is what I am. And this you know as you find it in Me.

But continue to pray. Continue to pray that those who have little oil will awaken, and those who have a little food will awaken and will come to Me. CRY OUT and spare not, for the days are short and the darkness cometh when no man will hear because of the darkness.

My Persecuted Church

Soon My whole Church will be the persecuted Church. It is the only Church of the End-Times. The persecuted Church — My remnant people — will be the only people that will be My glorious End-Time Church throughout the earth.

O I say, My children, walk with Me, talk with Me, confer with Me, live in Me, seek Me, worship Me, praise Me, pray fervent, effectual prayers. Oh, My people, do you not see that the day ahead is the day of the persecuted Church? Yes, all those who stand shall be in the persecuted Church!

I say, learn to come out of the world; learn to cast aside — cast off — all encumbrances; learn to be separated; learn to come into the secret closet of prayer to fellowship and love Me and listen to Me. Wait upon Me and hear Me speak unto you. For even as I am warning you in these Last Days, I am at the same time calling you. I am calling you, deep unto deep, because it is the call of these Last Days to come up and be seated in heavenly places, far above the circumstances. For you will live in circumstances that are like those you see in the persecuted Church even now. It will be the same.

There will be destruction on every side! There will be gross darkness; there will be death! There will be such darkness. But I say, in the midst of the darkness shall come forth My glory through a glorious people, a people who love Me and search for Me with all their hearts and find Me; and we are knit together, and I strengthen them with power in the inner man. And their joy is in Me, and their joy is to suffer for My sake. And they are never prisoners of the world, but they are prisoners of Mine. And they are willing to go the way of the Cross and deny themselves. And in the midst of darkness, in the midst of nothingness, in the midst of hunger and thirsting, they are filled with food — heavenly food. Even the ravens will feed them and will feed you when you walk that way.

By the Spirit, it is by the Spirit. Ask for the Spirit to teach you My ways, and ask for the Spirit to give you the revelation of My Word. Ask for the Spirit to be in control of you. Bow low before Me that I might lift you up and lead and guide you on the path of righteousness, that you might be that glorious Church, that humble glorious Church, through which I might show forth My glory. For I will not share My glory with any flesh; flesh must be crucified!

Come up! See the glory prepared for My people, My Church, My End-Time Church. For I am fashioning it, I am forming it in transformed lives right out of the midst of destruction. I am bringing it forth, raising it up. And so shall it be throughout the earth!

I tell you, My people, you shall not be spared persecution, but you shall be transformed — IF you will go the way of the Cross with Me, live with Me, abide with Me, and make of your hearts a cleansed and purified sanctuary wherein I might dwell.

The Righteous Remnant[64]

Hear Me, O My people, and listen to My words. You give attention continually to the words of men. You listen, read, you study and ponder and consider multitudes of words that express only the thoughts of others who, like yourself, are searching for truth. To search is not evil, but if you desire understanding, come directly to Me. Ask of Me. As the Scriptures teach, if any seeks wisdom, let him ask of God, for He gives liberally. [see James 1:5]

Wait upon Me, and I will clarify things that are dark and puzzling to you. Israel is My Chosen People, now as truly as in days of old. But like My Church has failed Me, even so has My People, Israel. There is, as there has always been, a wide discrepancy between what I have taught them, yes, even between what they believe, and what they experience . . . what they accept as My commandments, and what they do. You have both fallen short — Church and Israel alike!

But . . . I shall have those in whom I can rejoice — as I found pleasure in the devotion of David, and in the integrity of Job, yes, in the faith of the Shunammite, and the courage of Elijah. These lived in times when those who were truly dedicated to Me were in the minority, even as today. Goodness has never been a common commodity. Devotion and self-sacrifice have always been at a premium.

I shall have a people . . . but it will be the righteous remnant. *It will be no larger, percentagewise, than the family of Noah in the days of the flood!*

11. A Word for the Bride

You Ravish My Heart[65]

You ravish My heart, My promised bride; you ravish My heart! This day I invite you into the garden of My heart. It is there that I would teach you what it is to be yielded to My love. It is there that I would court you that you may know how much I love you and desire to call you to Myself.

I love you! I love you! I love you! You cannot hear these words too often, for they hold the truth that will transform you into the beautiful, perfect, radiant bride that I call you to be. (I, your Bridegroom, cannot hear these words too often from your lips, for they are the cords that bind your heart to My heart.) Yes, you know that I love you as your God, but you need to know that I love you with the love of a bridegroom for his beloved bride. I would have you gaze into My heart and see there the desire I have to belong wholly to you, so that you may belong wholly to Me. I, your Bridegroom, have pledged My love to you in good times and bad, for richer or for poorer, until death do we unite. In death you will find yourself in the arms of your Bridegroom, forever in the embrace of your God, forever in the eternal union of Love!

If you only knew how much you are loved. If you only knew the heart of your Bridegroom, the desire of the Bridegroom to hold you to His heart, to embrace you just as you are, to call you into that place where I can speak to your heart words of love that have been in My heart for all eternity. How I desire to hold you in My arms of love, arms that have been nailed to the Cross, that you might know My love for you.

My beautiful [child], still drag-racing the highways of the world in flight from your Divine Lover — you who have pursued the pathways of sin away from your God, you who have sought out a thousand things other than your God to find life and happiness — turn from those things and find in the arms of your Bridegroom all that can bring you happiness, both now and forevermore.

This day I invite you to stop running from Me, and to start running toward Me. In My arms you will come to know peace and rest. There you will hear words of love that you have never allowed yourself to hear. For the truth of all truths is: I, the King of kings and the Lord of lords, I who reign in the highest heavens and upon Earth, I who am Love, I AM IN LOVE WITH YOU!

Together let us discover the beauty that is within you — beauty not unlike the beauty within the heart of your God. You, My bride, are a reflection of the unlimited beauty of your Creator. Of all the created beauty in the world, there is no beauty like the invisible beauty of your soul. I CANNOT NOT love you as My bride. For this you were created. For this you were called into eternal existence that you might share forever the life of the Trinity, that you might share My Throne forever, that you might share in the mystery of the Eternal Nuptials.

In this is truth hidden from all ages but revealed to the churches and to you, My bride. There will never be a time when you, the bride, can say "I know it all!" No matter how learned your mind, how sharpened your gifts, there will always be infinitely more for you to know, infinitely more for you to experience.

You are living in the marvelous age of the courting of the bride and the coming of the Bridegroom. In it you will experience a growing desire to be courted, a growing knowledge of what it means to be courted by your God. When you say yes to My courting you, you say yes to a personal revelation of My bridal love for you. I call you this day to grow in a season of love and Divine courtship. I, your God, am here to love you, to embrace you, to hold your hand, to hold you to My heart.

I call you, My darling bride, for you are precious in My sight. You are the darling of My heart. I give you courage, My courage. I give you faithfulness, My faithfulness. I give you love, My love. You shall be My courageous, faithful, loving bride! For you have the courage, the faith, and the love of your Bridegroom pledged to you this day.

I will be for you all that you need Me to be. I will speak to you, and I will not grow weary. I will no longer be silent. You will hear the voice of your Bridegroom in the stillness of your heart. I have loved you from all eternity. I will love you for all eternity. I am madly in love with you! I have died that you might have life and know the love of the Bridegroom for the bride for all eternity. Where else in the world can you find such fidelity? Where else can you find such words of love, such promises of love, such love as I offer you this day? I am the Resurrection and the Life! You who believe in My love will never perish!

When you invite Me into the garden of your heart, I come in — not to concentrate on things not ready for My coming, but that I might open to you the vistas of My love. When you respond to My love with enthusiasm, you delight My heart! Be enthused for the ways I would reveal My love to you. Be enthused for the way I call you to celebrate My love. Not by might, not by power, but by My Spirit I will effect a massive change in the depths of your being. It will be a gentle work, for I am a gentle Lover.

I am also a jealous Lover. I do not tolerate Baals or idols. You, the bride, must make choices. If you choose light, the works of darkness must go. If you choose freedom, the unfreedoms must go. If you choose Me, then all that cannot come under My lordship must go. I cannot tolerate a bride that straddles the kingdoms. It is impossible to follow Me with one foot in each kingdom.

If you choose Me, you must be willing to be obedient to My love. You can no longer say Yes! No! Yes! Ask, and I will give you the grace to be My obedient bride, even as I am the obedient Son of My Father. This is a gift dear to the heart of your Bridegroom. I paid the price of My life for it. Do you want security, My bride? Be obedient and you will be secure in Me. Do you want freedom? Be obedient and you will know the liberty of the bride of God. You, the bride, whom the Son sets free, will be free indeed — free from the anxiety of knowing that you are doing the right thing, of knowing that you are in the right place, of knowing that you are using your gifts. Claim for your gift obedience to your Bridegroom, and all other gifts will be given to you besides.

Ask to see all the events of your life through the eyes of your Bridegroom. As you see through My eyes, you will see that there are many things that you thought you needed that you no longer need, for your treasure is in the heart of your Bridegroom. In My arms you will experience what it is to be totally wanted and to be totally loved. In My arms you, the bride, who have known abandonment, will be healed.

Bring Me your pain — pain in your subconscious and unconscious, pain felt in search of your healing. Bring all your pain and shattered dreams to the foot of My Cross, and you will know wholeness. There is no pain in the heart of the bride that was not first borne in the heart of your Bridegroom. You can never say to Me, your Bridegroom: "You do not know what it is to be abandoned."

As My bride, take your place at the foot of My Cross and experience My dying for you. Allow the power of Calvary's earthquake to strike the rock of all your unfreedoms, your paralyzed emotions, your unhealed psyche, your bondage to sin, the effects of generational sin in your life. Allow the full power of My death and My resurrection to set you free! Know the love of your crucified Bridegroom, and everything else will seem like so much rubbish!

12. The Final Call

The Way to Prepare

I'm giving you time and opportunity to clean and clear and get things ready. Detach yourself from the excess things in your life; they are a burden and a hindrance. They distract you from Me, My ways and purposes. Do not be greedy. Lay not up treasure on this earth, where moth and rust doth corrupt and thieves break through and steal. Set your heart and mind on the things above, where thieves cannot break through and steal. Make Me your greatest treasure! Seek Me as hidden treasure. There is oil and treasure in the house of the wise. Lay it up, store it up, hide it.

A STORM IS COMING, FAMINE IS COMING, DESTRUCTION IS COMING! All excess outward things will dissolve. Only that which is hidden in and with Me shall survive. Prepare, prepare! Even now the winds are beginning to blow! You need to tie things down in the Spirit, as it were. Lay them up, hide them, secure them, for the storm will be fierce! It will manifest itself in **wind, rain, floods, fire!**

Take precaution now, lay aside now, lay up treasure in Heaven now, hide in Me now, and you will stand strong on Me and in Me. The choice is yours. Yield to this cleansing, purifying, separating work I am doing now. Let My Wind and Water and Fire cleanse you now of all that would hinder you from being My cleansed, purified vessel. Seek Me daily in your secret closet and allow Me to search and know you. It is the way you prepare. It's the way you ready yourself.

The Last Hours

The last hours! And what will we do in these last hours? There is a cleaning and a purging that is going on now in the heart of the bride. Everything must be in a state of readiness. Everything must be set in order and prepared. There is a necessary trimming down, clearing out, and eliminating that is going on. It happens as you respond to the searching light of My Spirit. It happens as you are willing to face your sin in every area of your life. I demand truth in the inward parts. I demand purity in word, thought, deed, and action. There must be a carefulness in all you do. You must be willing to respond to Me and others according to the purity of My Word. You must be willing to be broken and harnessed. You must be willing to be identified with Me in truth and righteousness. Mercy must be at the very core of all that you do. If it is not, whatever you do will be for you and your gain, and not for Me and My Kingdom.

You are preparing to leave this world. Why do you hold so tightly to its things? Why do you continue to strive to be in control of everyone and everything? It is a prideful thing. It is not of My Kingdom.

Come, come, hold not back. The very things you fear to let go of and lay down, are the very things that will set you free — as you release them.

The thoughts of your heart must match the words of your lips, or you are a hypocrite and deceive yourself. Do not be like the Pharisees, who cleansed the outside of the cup and platter, but inside, *inside*, were ravenings and every evil work.

I love you. I desire to do this work of purifying and preparation in you. But you must come and know that NOW is the appointed time to separate, clean, clear, and make things right in every area and relationship. Be willing to die to yourself and take up your cross and follow Me. Come,

come, I will help you and teach you and assist you. Come, come, surrender all, yield to this breaking. It is the voice of the Bridegroom who calls you. Come, that your joy may be full. Come, that you may be ready when I come.

The Final Call

As the days draw to a close and the plan of the ages is fulfilled, I will come for My precious, purified, and spotless bride. Oh, how I long for her. Oh, how I long to have her close to My side, forever with Me, her Bridegroom and the Lover of her soul. Everything is ready; the call has gone forth: "Come, come, all things are ready. Come to the feast. Come to the marriage, the Marriage Supper of the Lamb. Do not delay!"

Answer the call of the Bridegroom to prepare and make yourself ready. Respond to His call of love. Respond to His wooing. Make no excuse! Set not your heart on other things. Do not be indifferent to this call. Come, come to the secret place and prepare your heart to be My bride. Cut all ties to earthly desires and loves so that you will be ready when you hear My final call to come — to come up and be with Me forever.

The wedding day draws near. Final preparations are being made. There is much excitement in Heaven! Oh, My love, My dove, hasten to the place of love and intimacy. Daily answer My call of love to prepare your heart. Listen, watch, and wait for the final call to arise, My love, My fair one; and come away.

Footnotes

1. Received by Gwen R. Shaw, "A Message From the Bridegroom to His Beloved," in *Angel Letter Number 4,* 1993; from End-Time Handmaidens, P.O. Box 447, Jasper, Arkansas 72641; p. 1

2. Given by Father Michael Scanlan, T.O.R., President, Franciscan University of Steubenville, Steubenville, Ohio 43952; at The National Committee Meeting of the National Charismatic Renewal; Jan. 1980.

3. Received by Gwen Shaw, "The Beginning of Sorrows: The Wrath of God is Beginning to be Poured Out," *Day by Day* by Gwen R. Shaw; Engeltal Press 1987, P.O. Box 447, Jasper, Arkansas 72641; pp. 229-231.

4. "Hard Times are Coming," from Heir Force Ministries, P.O. Box 26274, Wauwatosa, Wisconsin 53226, broadcasting on WKSH Radio.

5. "During the Holocaust," from Heir Force Ministries.

6. "Who Can Endure God's Anger," from Heir Force Ministries.

7. Received by Dumitru Duduman, "Examine Your Heart!" in *Hand of Help* newsletter, Vol. VII (1994), no. 1; Hand of Help Missions, P.O. Box 3494, Fullerton, California 92634; p. 3.

8. Received by Gwen Shaw, "Where are My Jeremiahs?" *End-Time Handmaidens Magazine,* February 1994, no. 44; P.O. Box 447, Jasper, Arkansas 72641; pp. 14-15.

9. Ron Auch, "Commentary," from his newsletter: *Pray-Tell Ministries,* November-December, 1993; P.O. Box 116, Kenosha, Wisconsin 53141; page 2.

10. Received by Gwen Shaw, "Come Out of the Harlot Church," *Daily Preparations for Perfection* by Gwen Shaw; Engeltal Press 1983, P.O. Box 447, Jasper, Arkansas 72641; p. 165.

11. Received by James P. Corbett, "Works of the Flesh," from Heir Force Ministries.

12. Received by James Corbett, "Early Morning Conversation," *Heir Force Herald,* September 1992; published by Heir Force Ministries, P.O. Box 26274, Wauwatosa, Wisconsin 53226; pp. 2-3.

13. "Who Will be Empowered," from Heir Force Ministries.

14. "To Overcome Sin," from Heir Force Ministries.

15. "Avoid Breaches," from Heir Force Ministries.

16. "Apply My Blood," *Prophecies of the End-Times* by R.C. Schaffter; The Clarion Call 1992, P.O. Box 335, Lannon, Wisconsin 53046; p. 115.

17. Received by Barbara Bloedow, "Overcoming the Enemy," *Prophecies of the End-Times,* pp. 116-117.

18. Received by Gwen Shaw, "The Blessing is in the Blood," *Day by Day,* pp. 406-407.

19. Received by Barbara Bloedow, "You Need Love Times," *Prophecies of the End-Times,* p. 97.

20. Received by Gwen Shaw, "You Can Spend Every Day of Your Life in My Courts," *Day by Day,* pp. 254-255.

21. Received by Charles Bernardi, "Tongues," *Perfect Way Newsletter,* P.O. Box 67, Highwood, Illinois 60040.

22. Received by Charles Bernardi, "Why Tongues?" *Perfect Way Newsletter.*

23. Received by Anna Schrader, *Prophecies of the Ages,* Vol. XI, pp. 25-26; also, *Prophecies of the End-Time;* now out of print, they were formerly published by: Christ For the Nations, P.O. Box 769000, Dallas, Texas 75376-9000; Freda Lindsay, Chairman of the Board. Reprinted by permission.

24. Received by Gwen Shaw, "Ask for Souls," *End-Time Handmaidens Magazine,* April 1992, no. 42, p. 21.

25. Gwen Shaw, "The Harvest is Waiting! Where are the Intercessors?" *End-Time Handmaidens Magazine,* April 1992, no. 42, p. 15.

26. Received by Barbara Bloedow, "You Do Not Understand About My Burdens," *Prophecies of the End-Times,* pp. 139-141.

27. Received by Gwen Shaw, "Revival or Revolution," *Day by Day,* pp. 256-257.

28. Received by Gwen Shaw, "Israel is His Beloved Pastureland," *Day by Day,* pp. 300-301.

29. Received by Gwen Shaw, "The Growth of Anti-Semitism," *End-Time Handmaidens Magazine,* May 1993, no. 43, p. 8.

30. Given by Millie Meehan during Succoth in Jerusalem in 1980, "The Holy Spirit Warns the Church of Its Anti-Semitic Spirit," printed in *End-Time Handmaidens Magazine,* May 1993, no. 43, p. 19.

31. Given by Lance Lambert, "Shaking the Nations," at Mount Carmel, Jerusalem; c/o Christian Friends of Israel, P.O. Box 1813, Jerusalem, Israel.

32. Given at Blue Mountain Christian Retreat, May, 1992 "Prophecy," *End-Time Handmaidens Magazine,* May 1993, no. 43, p. 19.

33. Received by Charles Bernardi, "Ye Expect to be Carried Away in My Rapture," *Perfect Way Newsletter.*

34. Received by Frances J. Roberts, "My Kingdom is at Hand," from *Come Away My Beloved* by Frances J. Roberts; King's Farspan, Inc. 1973, 1473 So. La Luna Avenue, Ojai, California 93023; pp. 158-159.

35. Received by Anna Schrader, *Prophecies of the Ages,* Vol. XI, p. 7.

36. Received by Anna Schrader, *Prophecies of the End-Time,* Vol. V, 7.

37. Received by Anna Schrader, *Prophecies of the Ages,* Vol. VIII, 9.

38. Received by Anna Schrader, *Prophecies of the End-Time,* Vol. II, 25.

39. Received by Anna Schrader, *Prophecies of the Ages,* Vol. IX, 17.

40. Received by Anna Schrader, Vol. XI, 3.

41. Received by Anna Schrader, *Prophecies of the End-Time,* Vol. III, 5.

42. Received by Anna Schrader, "It is More Wonderful to Fight Your Battles Beforehand," Vol. VII, 15.

43. Received by Anna Schrader, *Prophecies of the Ages,* Vol. X, 15.

44. Received by Anna Schrader, Vol. IX, 22.

45. Received by Anna Schrader, *Prophecies of the End-Time,* Vol. II, 30.

46. Received by Anna Schrader, *Prophecies of the Ages,* Vol. VIII, 8.

47. Received by Anna Schrader, Vol. XI, 6.

48. Received by Anna Schrader, Vol. X, 5.

49. Received by Anna Schrader, Vol. XI, 5.

50. Received by Anna Schrader, *Prophecies of the End-Time,* Vol. V, 30.

51. Received by Anna Schrader, *Prophecies of the Ages,* Vol. IX, 25.

52. Received by Dumitru Duduman, "Heavenly Visitors," (1991) from *Through the Fire Without Burning,* by Dumitru Duduman; Published by Virginia Boldea, Hand of Help, Inc., 1992, P.O. Box 3494, Fullerton, California 92634, (714) 447-1313; pp. 173-174.

53. Received by Dumitru Duduman, "Clouds in the Sky!" in *Hand of Help,* Vol. V (1992), no. 1, p. 1.

54. Received by Dumitru Duduman, "A Dream," in *Hand of Help,* Vol. VI (1993), no. 11, p. 4.

55. Received by Gwen Shaw, "Yet Seven Days . . . ," *End-Time Handmaidens Magazine,* Feb. 1994, pp. 8-9.

56. Received by Dumitru Duduman, "The Hand That Wrote on the Sky," in *Hand of Help,* Vol. VI (1993), no. 4, p. 1.

57. Received by Dumitru Duduman, "Letters to the Churches," in *Hand of Help,* Vol. VII (1994), no. 4, p. 3.

58. Received by Dumitru Duduman, "The Black Army," in *Hand of Help,* Vol. VI (1993), no. 5, p. 3.

59. Received by Gwen Shaw, "A Message of Love and Comfort from Jesus . . . ," *End-Time Handmaidens Magazine,* April 1992, no. 42, p. 14.

60. Received by Gwen Shaw, "The Hard and Bitter Trials of Life Reveal the Integrity of Your Soul," *Day by Day,* pp. 245-246.

61. Received by Dumitru Duduman, "Examine Your Heart!" in *Hand of Help,* Vol. VII (1994), no. 1, p. 3.

62. Received by Dumitru Duduman, "The Saviour Returns as Judge," in *Hand of Help,* Vol. VII (1994), no. 3, p. 2.

63. Received by Barbara Bloedow, "The Greatest Judgment Will Fall Upon My Church and My People!" *Prophecies of the End-Times,* pp. 74-75.

64. Received by Frances J. Roberts, "The Righteous Remnant," from *On the Highroad of Surrender* by Frances J. Roberts; King's Farspan, Inc. 1973, 1473 S. La Luna Avenue, Ojai, California 93023; p. 90.

65. Received by Sister Francis Clare, reprinted with permission of New Leaf Press, Inc. from *We, the Bride* by Sister Francis Clare; Copyright @ 1990 by New Leaf Press, Inc., Green Forest, Arkansas; chapter 12, pp. 91-98.

(Back of Order Page)

To Order Books

Additional copies of *The Last Call* can be purchased at your local Christian bookstore, or you may order them from:

The Clarion Call
P. O. Box 335
Lannon, WI 53046

Please send me_____copies of *The Last Call.*

Enclose $10.00 for each copy*
and for shipping add:

BOOK RATE:
1 - 2 books	$2.00
3 - 4 books	$3.00
5 - 6 books	$4.00
7 - 8 books	$5.00
9 and up	$6.00

or

FIRST CLASS MAIL (Priority Mail):
$3.00 for the first book and 75 cents for each additional book.

Make all checks or money orders payable to The Clarion Call.

Name: _____

Address: _____

City: _____ State: _____ Zip: _____

*Any order of ten or more books receives a discount.